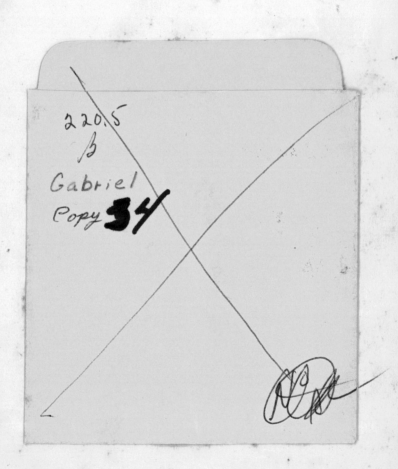

THE
BIBLE
STORY

A Textbook for use in the lower grades

NEW
REVISED EDITION

*With Suggestions
for Study by*

Sister M. Gabriel, O.S.F.

Sister Louis Mary, O.S.F.

REV. GEORGE JOHNSON, Ph.D.

MOST REV. JEROME D. HANNAN, D.D.
    Bishop of Scranton

SISTER M. DOMINICA, O.S.U.

BENZIGER BROTHERS, INC.
Printers to the Holy Apostolic See

New York, Boston, Cincinnati,
Chicago, San Francisco

THE
BIBLE
STORY

NIHIL OBSTAT:

Raymond T. Powers, S.T.D.
Censor Deputatus

IMPRIMATUR:

✠ Francis Cardinal Spellman
Archbishop of New York
April 19, 1960

The Nihil Obstat and Imprimatur are official declarations that a book or pamphlet is free of doctrinal or moral error. No implication is contained therein that those who have granted the Nihil Obstat and Imprimatur agree with the contents, opinions, or statements expressed.

PREFACE
TO THE
TEACHER

The Bible Story is intended to give children of the lower grades their first acquaintance with the stories of the Holy Bible. The biblical content selected for this book aims to present those major events of the Old and New Testament which can be comprehended by the young student.

The illustrations contained herein were drawn especially for this edition. They emphasize important phases of each story, and serve to impress the main points of the text in the child's mind. These illustrations also serve as visual aids in correlating religion with geography and history. A new revised *Teacher's Manual* accompanies the book.

A special feature of this new edition is the *Suggestions for Study*, designed by Sisters M. Gabriel and Louis Mary of the Franciscan Sisters of Peekskill, New York.

A WORD
TO BOYS
AND GIRLS

The Holy Bible is the greatest book in the world. It is the word of God. It is God's Book, and is divided into the Old Testament and the New Testament.

The Old Testament tells us about Adam and Eve and their fall in the Garden of Paradise. It tells us of God's promise to send a Redeemer. In the Old Testament, we read about God's Chosen People, the Israelites. They kept alive the worship of God and waited for the Redeemer.

The New Testament tells us much about the life of Jesus Christ, the Son of God, the Messias Who came into the world. It tells about His teachings, His death, His resurrection, and His Church.

While reading the stories in this book, always remember the wonderful gifts which God has given all men.

CONTENTS
The Old Testament

The New Testament

THE OLD TESTAMENT

I † THE
CREATION

In the beginning, there was no earth, no people, no animals, no plants nor trees. There was nothing, only God, for as you know God always was and always will be. It was God who created the world. By His almighty command, it came forth.

The Bible writer describes creation by dividing everything in the world into six days. In the first three days, God parted things. He parted the light from the darkness. He parted the waters of the sky from the waters of the earth. He parted the waters of the earth from the land.

During the next three days, God put things into the world. These things were the plants and flowers; the sun, moon and stars; the fishes of the sea; the beasts of the earth, and man.

When God made man, Adam, He made him in His

own image and likeness. God made man's body from the dust of the earth and gave him an immortal soul which will never die. God also made man ruler over all the earth.

God knew that what He had done was good and He blessed all that He had created. We always remember this by keeping one day a week especially holy. It is the day when we must rest from work. This day is Sunday.

Though the creation was a great act, God did not have to work at all to make it come about. He is not like your father who has to work hard to get food and clothes and make a home for his family. Maybe your father has to work five or six days a week to make a living. But God is all-powerful and by His almighty will He made the world out of nothing. He did not have to work to create the world. He created it by the power of His command.

SUGGESTIONS FOR STUDY

I. FILL IN THE BLANKS WITH THESE WORDS.

image　　God　　work　　world　　soul　　likeness

a. Before the creation of the world there was only
————.

b. God did not have to ———— to create the world.

c. God created the ———— by the power of His command.

d. God gave man an immortal ⸻.

e. God created man in His own ⸻ and
⸻.

2. ANSWER YES OR NO.

a. After the creation, did God bless all that He had created?

b. Did God have to work to create the world?

c. Do we rest from work on one day of the week?

d. Did God create man?

e. Did the Bible writer describe creation by dividing everything into six days?

3. DRAW A LINE UNDER THE CORRECT ANSWER.

a. God made man from (dust—a plant).

b. Man has a likeness to God chiefly because he has a (body—soul).

c. The soul will (die—never die).

4. HOW WELL CAN YOU THINK?

What day do we call holy and rest from work? How do we show God on that day that we love Him?

5. CAN YOU USE THESE WORDS IN SENTENCES?

creation	image	immortal
part	command	power
describe	almighty	likeness

5

II † OUR FIRST PARENTS AND THEIR CHILDREN

ADAM AND EVE IN THE
GARDEN OF PARADISE

When God created the first man, He placed him in a wonderful garden. This garden was the most beautiful spot on earth. It was so pleasant it has ever since been called the Garden of Paradise. This garden was filled with trees, plants and flowers of every kind. A river of sparkling clear, cool water flowed through it. Birds flew about and sang in the sunshine. Animals wandered everywhere and played together.

Adam knew all these animals and could play with them. He was not afraid of them and they were not afraid of him. No place on earth was ever as peaceful as this garden.

In the garden Adam could rest on the soft cool grass. He could eat the fruit that grew on the trees. God gave him only one command, and it seemed a very easy one to obey. "You may eat the fruit of every tree in Paradise," God said, "but you must not eat the fruit that grows upon the Tree of the Knowledge of Good and Evil. If you do, you shall surely die." Adam truly meant to obey, for he loved God very much.

Now, even though Adam had all the animals as companions, he grew lonely. The reason was that he had no companion like himself. God knew this and said, "It is not good for man to be alone," so He made woman, Eve, who was a human being just like Adam.

Both these people were very happy together in the garden. They both knew that they had to be obedient to God and keep His command. But this beautiful garden was not to remain peaceful. Its happiness was wrecked by the devil, who was once a good angel.

THE FALLEN ANGELS

When God created the angels, He gave them wonderful powers. They are spirits and have no bodies. But, to prove that they were worthy, God tested them and many angels fell away from Him. The one who we call the Devil led this revolt and so he was cast into hell with his followers.

The Devil hates God and tries to get men to hate God. People often think of the devil as a snake because he is so dangerous and sly.

One day the devil tempted Eve, "Why has God forbidden you to eat the fruit of every tree that grows in Paradise?"

Eve answered, "God has said that we may eat the fruit of every tree but one. He has forbidden us to touch the fruit that grows upon the Tree of the Knowledge of Good and Evil. If we eat it, we shall die."

"That is not true," the tempter replied. "You shall not die." And he started to coax Eve to eat the fruit, and kept suggesting to her that she would be as wise and great as God if she ate it.

Instead of being angry with the devil for trying to make her doubt God's word, Eve was foolish enough to listen. Eve wanted to be wiser than she was, so she took the fruit and ate it. She gave some to Adam, who also ate it.

The moment they had eaten the forbidden fruit, Adam and Eve knew that they had done something very wrong and they were no longer happy as they had been before. Instead, they were filled with shame and fear. They were even afraid of God, whom they loved. They trembled when they heard Him walking through the garden in the cool of the day. They ran and tried to hide themselves among the trees.

But God called, "Adam, where are you?"

Adam knew that he must answer when God called, so he came out from his hiding place and said, "I knew You were here, and I was afraid and hid myself."

"You were afraid," God answered, "because you have eaten the fruit that I forbade you to eat."

Adam bowed his head in shame. He tried to excuse himself by saying, "Eve gave the fruit to me and I ate it."

"Why have you done this?" God asked Eve.

She replied, "I was tempted and I ate the fruit."

To Adam and Eve God said, "Because you have disobeyed Me, you shall no longer be happy, you shall

know pain, and want, and sorrow. You shall no longer find your food without care, but you shall work for it. You shall earn your bread through the sweat of your brow and in the end you shall die and return to the dust from which I made you."

Although God forgave Adam and Eve, He punished them because they had disobeyed Him. He sent them out of the Garden of Paradise.

There never would have been any sadness in this world if Adam and Eve had obeyed God. It was this great sin that closed Paradise, and Heaven as well.

God then cursed the devil for tempting Adam and Eve to sin. From now on, there was to be war between all men and the devil. But this war was to end in victory for men because Jesus, Who is both God and man, would come to destroy the Devil's power.

CAIN KILLS HIS BROTHER ABEL

After Adam and Eve had been driven from Paradise, they had many children. Among the first were Cain and Abel. When they were grown up, Cain became a farmer and worked all day in the fields, plowing and gathering his crops. Abel became a shepherd and tended his flocks on the hillside and saw that no harm ever came to them.

One day Cain and Abel offered gifts to God. Abel's gift was a young lamb, one of the best and finest of his flocks. Cain's gift was some of the fruits of the earth, the finest which he had raised. They offered these gifts as sacrifices; that is, they burned them to show God that these gifts belonged to Him and that they did not wish to keep any part of them for themselves. In this way they thanked God for all that He had done for them and asked Him for His blessing.

Because Abel had a kind and loving heart, God was pleased with his gift and accepted it. He refused Cain's gift, however, for God knew that Cain did not do well, and was sinful.

God spoke gently to Cain, telling him that he would be rewarded in the same way as Abel if he did well, but that he would be punished if he sinned. Cain would not listen to God's warning. He hated Abel because God loved him, so one day he said, "Come, Abel, let us go for a walk in the fields."

Abel went with his brother. After they had walked for some distance and Cain knew that they could no longer be seen, he turned on his brother and killed him.

As soon as he had done this, he was terribly frightened and started to run away. But God, from Whom nothing can be hidden, called to him, saying, "Where is your brother Abel?" Cain answered, "I do not know; am I my brother's keeper?"

"Cain, Cain, what have you done?" God said, "Even now the voice of your brother's blood calls to Me from the earth for vengeance. Therefore, you shall be cursed upon the earth that has received your brother's blood. When you plow it, it shall no longer bring forth its fruits. And you shall be a wanderer upon the earth."

SUGGESTIONS FOR STUDY

1. FILL IN THE BLANKS WITH THESE WORDS.

forgave   shame   work   die   fear   obeyed

a. God told Adam and Eve that if they ate the fruit of the Tree of the Knowledge of Good and Evil they would _____.

b. After Adam and Eve had eaten the forbidden fruit they were filled with _____ and _____.

c. If Adam and Eve had _____ God, there never would have been any sadness in the world.

d. God said that Adam and Eve would have to _____ for their food.

e. God _____ Adam and Eve even though He punished them.

2. WHO AM I?

a. God accepted my sacrifice.
b. I tempted Adam and Eve.
c. I was jealous of my brother.
d. I refused Cain's gift.

e. I will come to destroy the power of the devil.

3. MATCH COLUMN I WITH COLUMN II.

a. Adam   ( ) was killed by his brother.
b. Eve   ( ) was cast out into hell.
c. Cain   ( ) meant to obey God's command.
d. Abel   ( ) coaxed Adam to disobey God.
e. The Devil   ( ) offered God the fruits of the earth.

4. WHO SAID THIS?

a. "Am I my brother's keeper?"
b. "I knew You were here and I was afraid and hid myself."
c. "I was tempted and I ate the fruit."
d. "You shall not die."
e. "Where is your brother Abel?"

5. HOW WELL CAN YOU THINK?

a. Adam and Eve sinned, and from that time on there were many sinful people in the world. Everyone born into the world has original sin on his soul. Which sacrament frees you from original sin?
b. God wants us to be happy, just as He wanted Adam and Eve to be happy. What must we do to be happy?

6. DO YOU KNOW WHAT THESE WORDS MEAN?

companion	tempter	wanderer
command	vengeance	forbade
curse	brow	flock

III † NOE AND THE GREAT FLOOD

Adam and Eve were very sad when they found out that Cain had killed his brother, and for a long time they mourned the death of Abel. To comfort them God sent them another son, whom they called Seth. Seth grew to be a kind and good man. He lived to be very old.

To live a long life is a blessing from God, and the better a person is, the more blessings he receives from God. The Bible tells us about a very good man named Mathusala, who lived longer than all the rest of Adam's descendants.

Many years went by since Adam and Eve were expelled from the Garden of Paradise, and their descendants spread over the land; and, like their first parents, they became sinful. God saw all this and said, "I will destroy man and wipe all living creatures that I have created from the face of the earth."

Now, there lived among these sinful people a man who still loved God and tried hard to do all that God wished him to do. This man's name was Noe. One day God spoke to Noe and said, "Behold, my children have become very wicked. They no longer seek Me or keep My commands. To punish them for their wicked ways, I will send down rain and there shall be a great flood. Every living creature and thing that I have created shall be destroyed. Only you and your family shall be saved, because you have loved and obeyed Me."

God then told Noe to build an ark of wood. God told him that it was to be very big. It was to have windows and a door, and was to be covered inside and out with pitch to keep out the water.

It took Noe and his three sons many years to build the ark. When it was finished, God told Noe to go into the ark and to take with him his wife and his sons and their wives. He was also to take along seven pairs of certain animals and one pair of all the other animals and living creatures as well as an abundance of food for his family and the animals.

Noe did all the things that God had commanded, and when everything was ready, Noe and his family and the animals entered the ark. They were now prepared for the terrible flood.

Before long, the rain began to fall in torrents, and it fell for days and nights. Never before had it rained so hard. The water rose rapidly and covered the trees and the houses. It lifted the ark high above the earth and it seemed to be floating on a great ocean. And still it rained and rained until the water covered the high mountains. Every creature that lived on the land—men, animals, birds—was destroyed.

After the rain had stopped, the water began to sink lower and lower until the ark, which had been floating, came to rest on the top of a mountain.

Noe waited for a while; then he opened the window of the ark and sent out a raven. The raven did not come back to him. He next sent out a dove, but the dove, finding no place to rest, returned to the ark.

After a week more had passed, Noe sent the dove out a second time. In the evening it returned to him carrying in its mouth a leafy olive twig. This was a sign to Noe that the waters had gone down below the tree tops. He waited a while longer before he let the dove go again. This time it did not come back at all, and Noe felt quite sure that the waters had disappeared. So Noe, with his wife, his sons, their wives and everything that was with him went out of the ark.

Noe was very grateful to God for having saved him and his family from the waters of the great flood. The first thing that he did after leaving the ark was to build an altar of stones. Upon it he offered a sacrifice of thanksgiving to God for having saved him and his family from the great flood.

God was pleased with the gifts that Noe offered and He promised Him that He would never again destroy the earth by water. He said, "As a sign of My promise I will place a rainbow in the heavens." Then God blessed Noe and his sons and gave them the world to live in and to rule.

SUGGESTIONS FOR STUDY

1. FILL IN THE BLANKS WITH THESE WORDS.

flood   destroyed   Noe   Mathusala   three

a. God told ——————— to build an ark.
b. Noe had ——————— sons.
c. To punish the wicked people God sent rain and there was a great ———————.
d. A good man named ——————— lived longer than all the rest of Adam's descendants.
e. Every creature that lived on the land was ———————.

2. ANSWER YES OR NO.

a. Was God pleased with the people who lived at the time of Noe?

b. Did the descendants of our first parents obey God and serve Him?

c. Was Noe's family saved because they loved and obeyed God?

d. Was Noe ungrateful to God for having saved him and his family?

e. Was God pleased with the sacrifice offered by Noe?

3. MATCH COLUMN I WITH COLUMN II.

a. Noe ( ) made of wood.
b. ark ( ) sign of a promise.
c. Seth ( ) blessed Noe.
d. God ( ) built the ark.
e. rainbow ( ) son of Adam and Eve.

4. DRAW A LINE UNDER THE CORRECT ANSWER.

a. We call Adam and Eve our (cousins—first parents).
b. The ark was (small—large).
c. The dove returned to the ark carrying (food—a twig).
d. God blessed the (world—Noe).
e. Noe (obeyed—disobeyed) God's commands.

5. HOW WELL CAN YOU THINK?

a. The first thing Noe did after leaving the ark was to thank God for His loving care. Name some of the ways in which God shows us His loving care.

b. Noe offered a sacrifice of thanksgiving and this pleased God. We also offer a sacrifice when we assist at Mass. Mention some things for which we must thank God.

6. CAN YOU USE THESE WORDS IN SENTENCES?

descendant	associate	grateful
torrents	struggled	gradually
mourned	wipe	disappeared

IV † ABRAHAM, FATHER OF THE CHOSEN PEOPLE

GOD'S PROMISE TO
ABRAHAM
M

any years after
the flood, there lived at a place called Haran a holy
man named Abram. Abram loved God with all his
heart. This pleased God and one day He spoke to
Abram and said, "Leave your country, your home,
your relatives and friends and come into the land
which I shall show to you. And I will make a great
people of you and I will bless you."

Although it was very hard for Abram to leave his
home and the friends he loved so dearly, he did as God
commanded. He took his wife Sarai, his nephew Lot,
and all his herds and flocks, and traveled for many
days. At last he came to a beautiful new country that
was filled with rich fields and pastures. This was the
Land of Chanaan, or as we call it, Palestine. Because it
was such a fruitful land, the Bible sometimes speaks of
it as "a land flowing with milk and honey."

In the Land of Chanaan, there was a place called Sichem, and here God again appeared to Abram. He said, "I will give this land to you and your children."

Abram was very grateful when he heard what God had promised and he immediately built an altar and offered a sacrifice of thanksgiving to God. Because of God's promises, the Land of Chanaan was called, from this time onward, "The Promised Land."

After Abram and his nephew Lot had been in Chanaan for some time, their herdsmen began to quarrel. Each wanted to get the best pasture land for his own flocks. Abram had many flocks; so had Lot, but the land in Chanaan was not so rich as to supply food for the flocks and herds of both.

Now, Abram was a peaceful man and when he heard that his herdsmen were quarreling with those of Lot, he called for Lot and said, "I beg of you, let there be no quarrel between you and me, for we are brethren. It would be better for you to leave me. If you will go to the left hand, I will take the right. But if you prefer the right, I will take the left."

Lot thought for a while. He knew that the plains of the river Jordan stretched far and wide and were very fertile. The city of Sodom lay close by. "I will go there," he said to himself, and immediately he prepared his family, his servants, his flocks, and all that belonged to him. He said good-bye to Abram and set out for his new home.

One day, after Lot had departed for Sodom, Abram heard the voice of God, Who said, "Lift up your eyes and look to the north and south, to the east and west. All the land that you see, I give to you and your descendants forever, and if any man can count the grains of dust upon the earth, he will be able to count your children. Arise and walk through this land, for it is now yours."

Abram always obeyed God's commands, so he moved his tents to Hebron and there built an altar to the Lord. He had now grown very old and, although God had blessed him and had given him great riches, he had no son to whom he might leave his goods and his lands when he died. He remembered that God had promised to send him a son and had told him that he would make him the father of a great nation. Abram knew that God always kept His word, so he waited patiently and prayed each day that God would fulfill this promise. One day, praying aloud, he said, "Lord God, I shall die without children and shall have to make the son of one of my servants my heir."

God heard his prayer and that night He called Abram out of his tent and said to him, "Look up to heaven and count the stars if you can. Behold, your children shall be as numerous as the stars and they shall inherit the land."

Abram listened and he believed all that God had said and trusted in Him. When God made this promise to Abram, Abram agreed to do what God wanted. We say that God made a covenant with Abram. It is like two people agreeing to go into a lasting partnership. This covenant was with Abram and his descendants. That is why they are called the Chosen People of God, and Abram is called the Father of the Chosen People.

Some time after this, God said to Abram, "Your name shall no longer be Abram but Abraham, because I have made you a father of many nations. And your wife's name shall no longer be Sarai, but Sara, for she shall be the mother of princes. For I will give you a son and I will bless him, and kings and nations shall descend from him. You shall call him Isaac."

ABRAHAM AND THE THREE GUESTS

Not long after these things had happened, Abraham was sitting one day at the door of his tent, for it was noon and very warm. Looking up, he saw three men standing near him. He said to the man who seemed to be their leader, "Sir, I beg of you, do not pass by my tent, but come and rest here in the shade of this tree while I bring water to wash your feet. My wife Sara shall have food cooked so that you can eat and refresh yourselves for the rest of the journey."

The three strangers seemed very happy to be made so welcome and while they rested, Abraham hastened to Sara and said, "Quickly, make some loaves on the hearth for our three guests." Then he went to the herd and chose a calf for the meal.

Soon the food was ready, and Abraham took the meat and the loaves and set them with milk and butter before the strangers. While they ate, he stood close by so that he could serve them.

After they had eaten, the strangers thanked Abraham, and one of them said to him: "I will return next year, and at that time Sara will have a son." When Abraham heard this, he knew that the stranger was God, and that His two companions were angels.

THE DESTRUCTION OF SODOM

When the guests were ready to continue their journey, Abraham walked with them to start them on their way. They walked toward Sodom, and as they traveled along, God told Abraham that He was going to destroy Sodom because the people who lived there had become wicked.

Abraham became very sad when he heard this, for Sodom was where Lot lived. Abraham drew nearer to God and begged Him to save the people, saying, "Will You destroy the good with the wicked? If there be fifty good people in the city, will they be punished with the wicked?"

"If I find fifty good people in Sodom, I will spare the whole city for their sake," God answered.

"What if there be forty-five good people there?" Abraham asked.

"For the sake of forty-five good people, I will save the city," God replied.

Abraham continued to plead for the people of Sodom. He asked God not to be angry with him for begging so hard, and then he pleaded with God to save the city, first for the sake of forty good people, then for the sake of thirty, then of twenty and, at last, even for the sake of ten.

God promised that He would save the city even if He found but ten good people living there. When He had said this, He left Abraham.

But there were not ten good people in Sodom. The only good people that could be found were Lot, his wife and their two daughters.

In the evening the two angels who had left Abraham came into the city of Sodom. They found Lot sitting at the gate of the city. As soon as Lot saw them he went forward to meet them, not knowing they were angels. He greeted them kindly and led them to his home.

Lot's wife and two daughters prepared a meal for the strangers and made them welcome. They begged the tired travelers to rest there for the night.

After the angels had eaten the meal, they said to Lot, "Take your wife and family away from the city, for God has sent us to destroy it."

At sunrise the next morning the angels arose and led Lot and his wife and his two daughters from the

city. They said to him, "Make haste, do not remain
on the plain, but flee to the mountain lest you too be
destroyed with those whom God is about to punish.
And as you go, do not look behind you."

As soon as Lot and his family were a safe distance
away, the Lord destroyed Sodom and all the people
who were in it.

ABRAHAM'S OBEDIENCE

Shortly after the destruction of Sodom, God kept
the promise that He had made to Abraham and Sara
and He sent them a son whom they named Isaac.

Isaac was a fine child and grew to be a strong, upright boy. His parents loved him very dearly.

When Isaac was almost grown up, God decided to test Abraham to see if he would be as obedient as he had always been, and if he loved God as much as he did his son, Isaac. One night, while Abraham slept, God called, "Abraham, Abraham."

Abraham knew at once that it was the voice of God speaking to him and he answered, "Here I am."

God said, "Take your son Isaac, whom you love so dearly, and go to a hill which I will show you and offer him to Me as a sacrifice."

It was a very hard thing that God asked Abraham to do. Abraham loved his son with all his heart, but he loved God even more. So, although his heart was breaking, he arose and prepared for the journey. He cut wood for the sacrifice and fastened it to the saddle of his ass. Then with Isaac and two servants he set out to find the mountain which God had said He would show him.

On and on they traveled for three days. Abraham was very quiet and sad. Isaac could not understand why his father was so unhappy and he tried in every way he could to cheer him, but it was no use.

On the third day they reached the hill which God had pointed out to Abraham, and he said to his two servants: "Remain here with the ass while the boy and I go up. When we have offered our sacrifice to God, we shall return to you."

Abraham took the wood and placed it on Isaac's shoulders. He himself carried a sword and fire in a bowl with which he would light the sacrifice.

As they were climbing up the mountain, Isaac said, "Father, we have fire and wood, but where is the victim for the sacrifice?"

"God will take care of that, my son. He will provide the victim," Abraham replied.

At last they reached the top of the hill and Abraham built a stone altar. He placed the wood on

it and then bound Isaac hand and foot and laid him on the wood. When all was done, he reached for his sword and was about to sacrifice Isaac when an angel called to him, "Abraham! Abraham! do not lay your hand upon the boy or harm him in any way. God only wished to test your love. He now knows that you love Him above all things and that for His sake you would not spare your only-begotten son."

Abraham's heart was filled with joy when he heard these words. Without delay he unfastened the cords that bound Isaac. Looking up, he saw a ram that was caught by its horns in some bushes nearby. He took the ram and offered it as a sacrifice to God in place of his son.

Once again the angel spoke to Abraham and said, "God will bless you and your children because you have obeyed His commands. And through you and your children all the nations of the earth shall be blessed."

A WIFE FOR ISAAC

Not many years after the angel had saved Isaac from the sacrifice, Isaac's mother died. Abraham and Isaac felt very sad, because they dearly loved Sara. She was buried in a tomb at Hebron.

Now Abraham was also growing old, and he wished to see Isaac happily married before he died. But Abraham was greatly troubled. The people of Chanaan did not believe in the one true God. Instead, they worshipped idols and were very wicked. He feared that his son Isaac might marry one of the women of Chanaan. So one day he called his servant Eliezer to him and said, "Go to my own country and choose a wife for my son Isaac from among my own people."

When Eliezer saw how troubled his master was, he set out immediately. He took ten camels and loaded them with rich gifts. Then he set out for the town where Abraham had once lived.

This town was a long way from Chanaan, and Eliezer traveled many days. When he came to the town, he made his camels lie down near a well that was outside the town walls. He himself sat close by. As he was sitting there, he prayed to God, saying, "O Lord, show kindness to my master Abraham. I know that the women of this town come to this well in the evening to draw water. To each of them I will say: 'Let down your pitcher that I may drink.' When I have spoken to the one whom You wish Isaac to marry, let her answer be: 'Drink, and I will also give water to your camels.' "

Eliezer had scarcely finished his prayer when a beautiful young girl came out to the well. She filled her pitcher and was returning to town when he stopped her and said, "Give me a little water to drink from your pitcher."

The maiden answered, "Drink, Sir," and she lowered her pitcher for him.

After he had finished drinking, she said, "I will draw water for your camels, too," and she filled her pitcher again.

When Eliezer heard these words, he could not speak for a moment or so. He felt that this girl was the very one whom God wished Isaac to marry.

He waited until she had given the camels all the water they wanted to drink. Then he gave her a pair of golden earrings and two golden bracelets. "Whose daughter are you?" he asked. "And, tell me, is there room in your house for me to rest for the night?"

The girl replied, "I am Rebecca, and my father was one of Nachor's sons. There is plenty of room in our house for you to stay and there is straw and food for your camels as well." Then she hastened to tell her family all that had happened.

Now, Eliezer knew that Rebecca's grandfather, Nachor, was Abraham's brother, and so Rebecca was related to Abraham. Eliezer was greatly pleased and he thanked God for answering his prayer.

When Rebecca reached home, she told about her meeting with the stranger. As soon as Laban, her brother, heard her story, he hurried out to meet Eliezer. He said to him, "Come with me, for we have room for you and for your camels."

Laban then led Abraham's servant into the house. Rebecca and her mother greeted him, while Laban took the packs off the camels and gave them food. The women brought Eliezer water to wash his feet and they set food before him. But he would not eat until he had first told them why he had come. He revealed to them who he was and in what manner

God had shown him that He wished Rebecca to be Isaac's bride.

When Eliezer had finished his story, he turned to Laban and said, "Tell me, what answer shall I carry to my master Abraham?"

To this, Laban replied, "The answer rests with God. What is there for us to say? Behold, my sister Rebecca stands before you. Take her and let her be the wife of your master's son as God wishes her to be."

As Eliezer listened to Laban's words, his heart was filled with joy. He brought out rich gifts and gave many of them to Rebecca. Others he gave to her mother and her brother.

Early the next morning he arose and prepared to return to Chanaan. Rebecca's mother and brother blessed her, and she and her nurse went with him.

Meanwhile, Isaac waited for Eliezer to return. One evening while he was walking in the fields, praying and thinking about God, he looked up and saw a cloud of dust in the distance. Soon he made out the shape of camels and he knew then that Eliezer was coming home.

When the travellers were near enough, Rebecca saw Isaac and quickly alighted from her camel. "Who is this man?" she asked Eliezer.

"It is my master Isaac," Eliezer replied.

The faithful servant then greeted Isaac and told him all that had happened.

Isaac loved Rebecca from the first moment he saw her. He and Abraham and their servants did all they could to make her happy and soon she and Isaac were married. Abraham lived with them for many years and gave his flocks and lands and all that he owned to Isaac, who took care of him in his old age.

Rebecca, too, was very kind to Abraham and when he died, Isaac buried him in a tomb in Hebron beside his wife Sara.

SUGGESTIONS FOR STUDY

1. WHO AM I?

    a. I was the only good man in Sodom.
    b. I am the father of the Chosen People.
    c. I was Isaac's wife.
    d. I was the child promised to Abraham.
    e. I went to find a wife for Isaac.

2. WHO SAID THIS?

    a. "Your children shall be as numerous as the stars."
    b. "My father, we have fire and wood, but where is the victim for the sacrifice?"
    c. "Will you destroy the good with the wicked?"
    d. "God will bless you and your children because you have obeyed His commands."
    e. "O Lord, show kindness to my master Abraham."

3. FILL IN THE BLANKS WITH THESE WORDS.

angels   Lot   son   Abram   Abraham

a. _____ was always obedient to God's commands.

b. The three strangers who came to visit Abraham were really two _____ and God.

c. Before God changed his name, Abraham's name was _____.

d. Abraham's herdsmen quarreled with the herdsmen of _____.

e. God had promised a _____ to Abraham.

4. MATCH COLUMN I WITH COLUMN II.

1. Promised Land	( )	Sodom
2. A wicked city	( )	Laban
3. Abraham's wife	( )	Eliezer
4. Rebecca's brother	( )	Chanaan
5. A faithful servant	( )	Sara

5. HOW WELL CAN YOU THINK?

a. Abraham always obeyed God's commands even though it was often hard to do so. Do we sometimes find it hard to obey God's commands?

b. God made Abraham wait until he was an old man before answering his prayer for a son. Why does God often make us wait before He answers our prayers?

c. Abraham was very kind to the three strangers, even though he did not know who they really were. Why should we be kind to others?

6. DO YOU KNOW WHAT THESE WORDS MEAN?

herdsmen	heir	hearth
plain	descend	partnership
lonely	idols	reveal

V † ESAU AND JACOB, TWO BROTHERS

For nearly twenty years, Isaac and Rebecca had no children. Then God heard their prayers and sent them two sons. The elder was called Esau and the younger Jacob. Esau was large and strong. His skin was rough and hairy. He loved to be out in the open and spent much of his time roaming through the woods and fields. When he was grown, he became a farmer and skillful hunter. Isaac loved Esau because he was strong and fearless, and he enjoyed eating the meat that Esau brought from the hunt.

Jacob was quite different from his brother. His skin was soft and smooth. He was very quiet and liked to stay at home. When he grew old enough, he became a shepherd. Because of his quiet ways, his mother, Rebecca, loved Jacob more dearly than she did her older son, Esau.

One day Esau came home from the fields tired and hungry. He saw his brother cooking some food over the fire and he said to him, "Give me some of that food, for I am very hungry."

Jacob answered, "I will give it to you if you will sell me your birthright."

Now, in those days the oldest son always received his father's last blessing. Besides this, he became the head of the family after his father died and received the largest part of what his father owned. The father's last blessing and the largest share of his property were called the birthright of the first-born. Since Esau was the first-born, the birthright belonged to him.

Esau was very much surprised when he heard Jacob's answer. He thought for a moment, and then he said, "If I die of hunger, what good will a birthright do me?" He sold it to Jacob, ate the food and went his way. Esau valued his birthright very lightly.

One day, when Isaac had grown so old that he could scarcely walk, and his eyes had grown so dim that he could not see, he called Esau to him and said, "Esau, my son, you see that I have grown very old and I do not know how long I shall live. Go out into the fields once more and when you have killed an animal, cook it for me the way I like it, and bring it here so that I may eat and bless you before I die."

Now, Rebecca was in the next room and heard all that Isaac said to Esau and it troubled her. She wished Jacob to receive his father's blessing. She waited until Esau had gone into the fields to hunt; then she called Jacob and told him what Isaac said. She said, "Now, son, go and bring me two of the finest young goats from the flock. I will cook them the way that pleases your father most, and you will carry the meat to him so that he will eat it and bless you instead of Esau."

"But," Jacob said to his mother, "Father will know at once that I am not Esau, for Esau's arms are hairy, while mine are not. If he finds me out, he will curse me instead of blessing me."

To this, Rebecca answered, "I will take care of that, my son. Only do as I command."

So Jacob went out to the flocks and chose two of the finest young goats. When he had killed them, he brought them to his mother and she cooked them.

She took Esau's best clothes and dressed Jacob in them and she covered his hands and neck with the skins of the young goats. Then, she gave him the meat and some bread and sent him to Isaac.

As Jacob went into his father's room he said, "My father."

Isaac answered, "Which of my sons are you?"

Jacob replied, "I am Esau, your first-born; I have

done as you commanded; come, eat the meat that I have brought you and give me your blessing."

"How could you find an animal so quickly, my son?" Isaac said. "Come here and let me feel you, so that I may know whether or not you are Esau."

Jacob drew close to his father and, as Isaac touched the hairy skin that covered the lad's hands, he said, "The voice is the voice of Jacob but the hands are the hands of Esau." Finally, Isaac believed that this was Esau and he took the meat that his younger son had brought him. When he had eaten it, he blessed him, saying, "May God give you full and plenty of the good things of the earth; may He let people serve you and tribes respect you; may all who bless you be blessed, and those who curse you be cursed."

Jacob had scarcely left his father's room when Esau came in carrying the meat of the animal that he had caught and cooked. "Come, father, eat and give me your blessing," he said.

When Isaac heard Esau's voice, he turned toward him in surprise and asked, "Who are you?"

Esau answered, "I am Esau, your first-born."

Then Isaac said to Esau, "Before you came, your brother Jacob brought meat to me and when I had eaten, I blessed him. He deceived me and got your blessing."

Esau's heart was broken when he heard this. Falling upon his knees, he wept bitterly and said to his father, "Have you, then, no blessing for me?"

Isaac felt very sorry for Esau and he blessed him. This blessing, however, was not the blessing of the first-born.

Esau was very angry with Jacob and he held a grudge against him for having received his father's blessing. He said, "When my father is dead, I will kill Jacob."

JACOB FLEES FROM ESAU

Rebecca heard Esau and saw how angry he was. She sent for Jacob and said, "Your brother Esau is very angry because your father has given you his blessing. I fear that he will kill you. Flee to Haran, where my brother Laban lives, and stay there with him. After Esau's anger has passed and he has forgotten what you have done, I will send for you and you can return."

Jacob got ready to depart for Haran. He said good-bye to his father, and Isaac blessed him a second time and told him to seek a bride among the daughters of Laban. Jacob set out and traveled for many days. One evening he stopped to rest in an open field.

Feeling weary after the long day's journey, he lay
down on the ground to rest. He took one of the stones
from the field and placed it under his head, using it
as a pillow. That night he had a strange dream. He
dreamed that he saw a great ladder reaching from the
earth all the way up to heaven. Many angels were
moving up and down the ladder. Suddenly, he saw
God Himself standing beside him, and God said to
Jacob, "I am the Lord, the God of Abraham and
Isaac. The land where you are sleeping I will give to
you and to your children. And your children shall
be as numberless as the grains of dust on the earth,
and through you and your children all nations shall

be blessed. Wherever you go, I will go with you and watch over you and bring you back to this land."

When Jacob awoke, he remembered his dream and rejoiced. He said to himself, "Surely, the Lord is in this place and I did not know it."

Then he arose and, taking the stone upon which his head had rested, he poured oil on it and set it up as a sign that the place belonged to God. He called the place Bethel, which means House of God. He also made a vow, saying, "If the Lord shall guide me and return me safely to my father's home, then the Lord shall be my God and I will give Him a tenth part of all that He has given me."

JACOB MARRIES RACHEL

In the morning Jacob traveled on toward Haran. Soon he came to a well around which three flocks of sheep were lying. Going up to the shepherds who were standing close by, he asked them if they knew Laban. One of the shepherds pointed to a young girl who was coming down the road. She was driving sheep to the well. "That is Rachel, the daughter of Laban," the shepherd said.

When Rachel came near, Jacob pushed away the stone that covered the mouth of the well and helped her to water her flock. He told her that he was the son of Rebecca, her father's sister.

Rachel was very happy when she heard that Jacob was her cousin. She hurried home to tell her father about him. The news that his sister's son was coming filled Laban with joy. He rushed out to meet him and welcomed him to his home.

Jacob told Laban why he had come and why his mother did not wish him to return to Chanaan until she sent for him. "Can you give me work as a shepherd?" he inquired.

"What wages would you want for your services?" Laban asked.

Jacob replied, "I will serve you seven years without wages or any other reward if you will give me Rachel to be my wife." Laban agreed.

For seven years Jacob worked faithfully for Laban. But when the seven years were up, Laban did not keep his promise. He gave Jacob Rachel's sister, Lia, for his wife instead of Rachel.

Now, Jacob loved Rachel, so he said to Laban, "You promised to give me Rachel for my wife. Why have you given me her sister?"

Laban replied, "Lia should·be married first, for she is older than Rachel. That is why I have given her to you. If you promise me that you will remain seven years longer with me, within seven days I will give you Rachel."

Jacob could not bear to think of leaving Rachel, so he promised to do as Laban asked. And when seven days had passed, Laban gave Rachel to Jacob.

After Jacob married Rachel, he worked for Laban for many years. During these years God blessed Jacob and he became very rich. When Laban saw how rich Jacob had become, he grew jealous. He tried to cheat Jacob out of that which rightfully belonged to him.

But, one night, as Jacob slept, God spoke to him and said, "Arise, leave this land and return to your own country. I will go with you to protect you."

Jacob arose without delay. He gathered together what belonged to him and started back to Chanaan and to Isaac his father.

It happened that Laban was away in the country at this time, shearing his sheep. Several days passed before he learned that Jacob had left. When at last he did hear of it, he was very angry and made up his mind to follow Jacob and bring him back.

Laban had to travel seven days before he came to the place where Jacob and those that were with him were resting. As he was about to enter Jacob's camp, God spoke to Laban and said, "Take care that you do not speak harshly with Jacob."

Laban obeyed God, and when he and Jacob talked together, Jacob promised that he would forget all the trouble Laban had caused him. Laban promised that he would always be friendly with Jacob. To help them remember their agreement, Jacob piled up a heap of stones to serve as a reminder and they ate near it. That same evening Laban returned home.

ESAU FORGIVES JACOB

The next morning Jacob traveled on toward Chanaan. When he reached the banks of the river Jordan, he grew worried. He remembered that his brother Esau hated him and he was afraid to meet him. So he sent messengers on to carry gifts to Esau and to ask his forgiveness. Soon the messengers returned to Jacob and said, "Esau is coming to greet you, and with him are four hundred men."

When Jacob heard this, he was filled with fear and sadness. He was sure that Esau was still angry and that he was coming to destroy his flocks and to kill him and all that were dear to him. He said to himself, "I will divide my people and my flocks into two companies and if Esau destroys one, the other will escape." Jacob fell on his knees and prayed to God for help, saying, "O God of my father Abraham, and God of my father Isaac, save me, I beg of You, from the wrath of my brother Esau, for I fear that he will kill me and my dear ones. Remember when You commanded me to return to this land, You promised to watch over me."

That night Jacob was troubled. He watched and prayed alone. Suddenly a stranger appeared in the darkness and grabbed him. The stranger tried to throw him to the ground and the two wrestled and struggled for a long time. Finally, when it began to grow light, the stranger said, "Let me go, for it is the break of day." But Jacob answered, "I will not let you go until you bless me."

"What is your name?" the stranger asked.

Jacob answered, "It is Jacob."

The stranger said, "You shall no longer be called Jacob, but Israel." Then he blessed Jacob and disappeared, and Jacob knew that he had wrestled all night with an angel. He knew, too, that this was a sign that God would protect him against Esau.

Early that morning Jacob saw Esau and his men coming toward him and he arranged all the people of his household to meet his brother. Those he loved dearest he placed behind all the rest. Then he himself went forward and bowed very low as Esau came near.

As soon as Esau saw Jacob, he rushed to him and threw his strong arms about his neck. The two brothers kissed each other and wept for joy.

After Esau had greeted his brother, he looked about and saw the women and children. He asked, "Who are they?"

Jacob replied, "They are the children whom God has given me."

Then Jacob called to the women and children and they drew near to Esau and bowed down before him.

Jacob now offered many gifts to Esau, but Esau refused them, saying, "I have plenty, my brother; keep what you have for yourself." But Jacob would not let Esau refuse the gifts. He begged him to accept them. Esau, in order to prove that he was no longer angry, accepted the gifts and thanked Jacob for them.

Esau went back the way he had come and Jacob continued on his journey. At last Jacob came to Hebron, where Isaac, his aged father, lived. Here he remained until Isaac died. Then he and Esau buried Isaac beside his father Abraham and his mother Sara.

SUGGESTIONS FOR STUDY

1. FILL IN THE BLANKS WITH THESE WORDS.

promise   shepherd   Jacob   birthright   Laban

a. Esau sold his ——————— for food.
b. The blessing of the first-born was given to ———————.
c. Jacob fled to the house of ———————.
d. God made Jacob a ——————— in a dream.
e. Jacob asked Laban to give him work as a ———————.

2. ANSWER THESE QUESTIONS.

a. Who became angry at his brother?
b. Which son deceived Isaac?
c. Who told Jacob to return to his own country?
d. Why was Jacob afraid to return to Chanaan?
e. Who became the wife of Jacob?

3. WHO AM I?

a. I am the mother of Esau and Jacob.
b. My brother dressed in my clothes and received a blessing.
c. I gave my daughter Rachel to Jacob in marriage.
d. I wrestled all night with Jacob.
e. My name was changed to Israel.

4. WHO SAID THIS AND TO WHOM?

    a. "Through you and your children all nations shall be blessed."

    b. "Surely the Lord is in this place and I did not know it."

    c. "Have you, then, no blessing for me?"

    d. "The voice is the voice of Jacob but the hands are the hands of Esau."

    e. "I will give it to you if you will sell me your birthright."

5. HOW WELL CAN YOU THINK?

    a. God promised Jacob that "through your children all nations shall be blessed." Which of Jacob's descendants brought the greatest blessings to the whole world?

    b. Jacob prayed to God: "You commanded me to return to this land, You promised to watch over me." Does God watch over you? Tell some ways in which you know He is watching over you.

    c. Esau was very angry at his brother, but he forgave him. How can we imitate Esau and so please God?

6. CAN YOU USE THESE WORDS IN SENTENCES?

birthright	skillful	inquire
deceived	wrestled	envious
grudge	reminder	grabbed

VI † JOSEPH
IN EGYPT

Whaen Jacob returned to Chanaan, Benjamin, the youngest of his twelve sons, was but a baby. Joseph, the next youngest son, was a lad of sixteen. The other sons were grown men. They worked all day in their father's fields, planting and gathering the grain and tending the flocks.

Jacob loved all of his sons, but he loved Joseph best and gave him a beautiful coat of many colors. Joseph was very proud of this fine coat, but his brothers were angry when they saw it on him. Their coats were made from the rough skins of animals, while Joseph's was like that of a prince. They became jealous of their younger brother because they saw that their father loved him more than he loved them.

One night Joseph had a strange dream. He dreamed that he and his brothers were in the fields tying up bundles, or sheaves of grain. Suddenly his sheaf stood upright, and all his brothers' sheaves gathered around and bowed down before it.

When Joseph told the dream to his brothers, they grew angrier. They thought that the dream was a sign that Joseph would rule over them and they would have to bow down before him.

Then Joseph had another dream. He told this dream to his father as well as to his brothers. He said, "In my dream I saw the sun, the moon and eleven stars bowing before me."

Jacob was not pleased when he heard what Joseph said. He scolded him and asked, "What does this dream mean? Shall I, your mother and your eleven brothers bow down to the ground before you?"

As the brothers listened to this dream, they murmured against Joseph and they began to hate him. Jacob, however, never forgot the dream. He wondered if it was really a message from God and if it would come true.

Some time later, the brothers took their flocks to a pasture many miles from their home in Hebron. Joseph remained at home with his father and his youngest brother Benjamin. Jacob often thought of his older sons and wondered how they were getting along. One day he called Joseph to him and said,

"Your brothers are feeding their flocks in Sichem. Go and see if things are well with them and the flocks. Bring me back word."

Joseph obeyed at once. He left Hebron and went to Sichem. When he got there, he wandered about in the fields looking for his brothers, but he could not find them anywhere. At last he met a man who told him that his brothers had gone on to Dothain with their flocks. So Joseph went to Dothain and there he found his brothers.

When the brothers saw Joseph coming toward them in his coat of many colors, they said to each other, "Here comes the dreamer. Let us kill him and cast him into some old well. We will say a wild beast has devoured him."

Now Ruben, the oldest of Jacob's sons, was very sad when he heard what his brothers said. He did not want them to kill Joseph and he said to them, "Do not kill the boy; do not shed his blood. Throw him into this well here in the wilderness."

Ruben said this to save Joseph from the hands of his older brothers. He thought to himself, "When the others have gone, I will return and take Joseph out of the well and bring him safely back to our father."

When Joseph came up to them, his brothers grabbed him and stripped off his brightly colored coat. They carried him to the well nearby, and threw him into it. Fortunately for Joseph, the well had no water in it or he would have been drowned. The brothers then decided to sit down and eat their noon-day meal.

While the brothers were eating, some merchants who were on their way to Egypt passed by. When Juda, one of the brothers, saw them, he said to the others, "What shall we gain if we kill Joseph or let him die in the well? Besides, he is our brother. Come, let us sell him instead to these merchants."

The brothers took Juda's advice. They pulled Joseph out of the well and asked the merchants how

much could be gotten for him. The merchants offered them twenty pieces of silver. The brothers were satisfied with this sum, so the merchants took Joseph with them and traveled on.

Ruben, who had not been present, returned to the well. He called and called, but there was no answer. Ruben wept and tore his garments in misery, for he knew that his father would blame him for any harm that should come to Joseph. He hurried after his brothers and said, "The boy is gone. What shall I do?"

The brothers did not know what to tell their father, Jacob about Joseph. They talked together and at last they thought of a plan to save Ruben and themselves from their father's wrath. They took Joseph's coat of many colors and dipped it in the blood of a young goat which they had killed. Then they sent someone with the bloodstained coat to their father.

Jacob knew at once that the coat was the one that he had given to Joseph. He wept and cried aloud, "It is my son's coat. A wild beast has eaten him. A beast has devoured Joseph."

Jacob's heart was broken. For a long time he mourned and wept for the son he loved. Although his children tried to comfort him in every way they could, he was still very sad, and he never forgot his son, Joseph.

When the merchants reached Egypt, they sold Joseph to Putiphar, a captain in the king's army. Now, God was with Joseph and He blessed him in all he did. When Putiphar saw that Joseph was very bright, he gave him charge over his servants, his fields, his goods and his cattle. Then God blessed the house of Putiphar and he soon became very rich.

Joseph was happy in his master's house and everything went well. But then the wife of Putiphar became angry with Joseph and she told her husband a lie about him. Putiphar believed her and had Joseph put into prison.

Though Joseph was put into prison he trusted in God and God still blessed him. Soon the chief prison keeper grew to like him and gave him charge over all the other prisoners.

While Joseph was in prison, the king became angry with two of his servants and they too were cast into prison. One of these men was the king's chief baker and the other was his chief butler. Joseph was given charge over them and he tried to comfort them. But one morning when he came to them, he found them looking sadder than they usually looked. "What is the matter, why do you look so sad today?" he asked.

They answered, "Each of us had a dream last night and we do not know what our dreams mean."

"Do you not know," said Joseph, "that the power to explain dreams comes from God? Tell them to me and perhaps God will help me explain them to you."

The chief butler spoke first. He said, "I dreamed that I saw a vine. On the vine there were three branches. The branches first sprouted buds and then blossoms. Then the blossoms sprouted ripe grapes. I held the king's cup in my hand. I took the grapes and pressed them into the cup and gave it to the king."

Joseph said, "I will explain the dream for you. The three branches are three days. After three days the king will send for you. He will give you your place again and you shall present him with his cup just as you did before. Remember me when you are with the king and ask him to take me out of this prison."

Then the chief baker told his dream. "I dreamed," he said, "that I had three baskets on my head. The top basket was filled with all kinds of bread and cake. And the birds of the air came and ate out of it."

"This is the meaning of your dream," Joseph said. "The three baskets are three days. After three days the king will send for you. He will cut off your head and hang you upon a gallows and the birds shall come and eat your flesh."

The king's birthday fell on the third day after Joseph had explained the dreams. The king made a great feast. During the feast he thought of the chief butler and the chief baker who were in prison and he sent for them. He gave the chief butler his place again, but he hanged the chief baker.

The chief butler was so happy when he was returned to his place that he forgot all about his promise to Joseph. So Joseph remained in prison.

Two years later, the king was annoyed with strange dreams. He sent for all the wise men of his kingdom, but no one could tell him what the dreams meant. When the chief butler saw all these men coming to the palace, he remembered Joseph, who was still in prison, and he said to the king, "While the chief baker and I were in prison, we each had a dream. A young Hebrew who was there told us what they meant and all that he said came true."

When the king heard this, he sent for Joseph. The king said to him, "I have dreamed strange dreams and there is no one who can explain them to me. I have heard that you are very wise. Can you tell me what they mean?"

Joseph answered, "Only God can tell you what dreams mean. But perhaps He will give me the power to explain your dreams."

Then the king told Joseph what he had dreamed. He said, "I stood on the bank of a river and out of the river came seven fat, beautiful cows. They grazed along the river. Then, out of the river came seven thin and ugly cows, the like of which I have never seen in Egypt. And the seven thin and ugly cows ate up the fat, beautiful cows, but after they had finished, they were as lean as ever.

"I was frightened and I awoke. But after a while I fell asleep again and dreamed another dream. I dreamed about seven ears of corn which grew on one stalk. They were full and very fine. Then I saw seven other ears growing on the same stalk. They were thin and dry and shrunken. The seven thin ears then ate up the seven fat ears."

After Joseph had listened to the king's dreams, he said, "I will tell you what your dreams mean. The two dreams mean the same thing. They are a message that God has sent to tell you what is going to happen. The seven fat cows and the seven full ears of corn are seven years of plenty. The seven lean cows and the seven thin ears are seven years of famine. There will be seven years of plenty in Egypt. Then will follow seven years of famine when all the crops will fail.

"Now, let the king choose a wise man to take charge of the land of Egypt. And let this man store

up food during the seven years of plenty so that the people will have something to eat during the seven years of famine."

Joseph's words pleased the king and he said, "Since God has shown all this to you, where shall I find one who is wiser? I will make you head over my house and all the people shall obey you. No one shall be above you but myself."

The king took off his own ring and put it on Joseph's finger. He dressed him in linen robes and hung a golden chain about his neck. He then sent him to ride through the streets of the city in one of his own chariots. And wherever Joseph went, a soldier

ran on before him calling out, "Bow to Joseph, for he has been made governor over all Egypt."

The seven years of plenty came just as Joseph had said they would. The harvests were rich and large. During those years Joseph told the people to store away as much food as they could. Meanwhile, he gathered and put away in great storehouses part of all the crops that were raised in Egypt.

When the seven years of plenty passed, there came seven years of famine. The famine spread to other countries. The people of Egypt cried out to their king for food, and he said to them, "Go to Joseph and do whatever he commands you to do."

As soon as Joseph heard the cries of the hungry people, he ordered his servants to open the great storehouses that were still filled to their very roofs. Then he commanded them to sell food to all who came to buy.

It was not long before the news that there was food to be had in Egypt spread to other lands. Strangers then came from near and far to buy grain.

JOSEPH AND HIS BROTHERS

The famine was very great in the Land of Chanaan, where Jacob and Joseph's brothers still lived. When

Jacob heard that there was food in Egypt, he said to his sons, "Go there and buy grain for us or we will starve to death."

So ten of Joseph's brothers set out for Egypt to buy grain. Jacob would not let Benjamin, his youngest son, go with them, for he feared that some harm might come to him on the way.

After many days' travel the brothers reached Egypt and, going to the palace where Joseph lived, they bowed low before him. They did not know that this man was their brother whom they had treated so cruelly.

As soon as Joseph saw his brothers, he knew them, but he did not wish them to know him. He wanted first to learn whether or not they remembered and hated him as much as they did when they sold him to the merchants. He spoke roughly to them as if they were strangers and asked, "From what country do you come?"

"We come from Chanaan to buy food," the brothers answered.

Joseph pretended that he did not believe them and he said, "You are spies who have come to look about our land."

The brothers were frightened when they heard this and they replied, "We are not spies, but honest men.

Our father sent us here to buy grain, for there is no food in our land."

Now Joseph wished to hear more about his father, so he said, "Who is your father? Where is he now?"

They answered, "Our father is Jacob. He is at home with our youngest brother Benjamin. We had another brother named Joseph, but he is dead and our father still mourns for him. That is why he would not let Benjamin come with us."

Joseph still pretended that he did not believe his brothers and he ordered them to be put into prison. After three days he sent for them and said, "I will keep only one of you in prison. You others may return to your home in Chanaan with the food that you have bought. But you must return and bring me your youngest brother so that I may know that you have told the truth. If you do not return, you will never again see the brother who is to remain here with me."

The brothers were very sad when they heard what Joseph said, and they talked to each other in their own language. They did not know that Joseph could understand them. They said, "We deserve this punishment because we were so cruel to Joseph. He begged us not to sell him to the merchants, but we would not listen to him. Now we are being punished."

As Joseph listened to what his brothers said, he pitied them. He knew now that they were sorry for what they had done, and he went out so that they would not see him and wept. When he returned, he ordered Simeon, one of the brothers, to be bound hand and foot and cast into prison while the others looked on. Then he commanded his servants to fill their sacks with grain and to hide in the top of each sack the money which they had given to pay for it. He also gave them food for their journey.

So the nine brothers loaded the asses with the grain and food which Joseph had given them and returned to Chanaan. When they reached there, they told

Jacob all that had happened in Egypt. They opened their sacks to show him the grain that they had brought. And, behold, there was the money in the top of each sack! This frightened them, for they did not know how the money came to be there.

Jacob was very sad when he heard that Simeon was in prison, but he would not at first permit the brothers to take Benjamin back with them. He said, "Joseph is dead and if any harm should come to Benjamin, I will die."

When most of the grain which Joseph had given them had been eaten, Jacob said to his sons, "Go again to Egypt and buy more food."

"We will go if you will let Benjamin go with us," Juda replied. "But we cannot go without him. The governor will not see us. Let me take the boy and do not fear, for I will care for him and bring him safely home to you."

"What else is there to do?" Jacob said, at last. "If we have no food, we shall all starve. There is no time to lose. Go at once and take Benjamin with you. And take, also, not only the money you found in your sacks, but twice as much as what you took before so that you will have enough to pay for the grain."

It did not take the brothers long to prepare for the journey. When they were ready to depart, Jacob blessed them and begged God to let them return safely to him together with Benjamin and Simeon.

When Joseph saw his brothers, he was well pleased and he made a great feast for them. His heart was filled with joy when he saw Benjamin and he asked, "Is this your young brother of whom you told me?"

The brothers said that this was Benjamin, and Joseph blessed the boy, saying, "May God be with you, my son."

While his brothers were eating, Joseph said to one of his servants, "Fill the men's sacks with as much grain as they will hold and put back into them the money given to pay for the grain. Put also my silver cup in the top of Benjamin's sack."

The servant did as Joseph had ordered and, when morning came, the brothers set out for home once more. Simeon went with them. When they had gone, Joseph called his servant to him and said, "Ride after the men and, when you have overtaken them, stop them and say, 'Why have you returned evil for good? Why have you stolen the governor's silver cup after all he has done for you?'"

The servant hurried after them and overtook them when they were but a short distance from the city. He stopped them and asked why they had stolen the governor's silver cup.

The brothers were angry when they heard what the servant said. "We have not stolen it," they said. "Search our sacks and see for yourself. If you find it, he in whose sack it is hidden shall return and be your master's slave."

Saying this, they unloaded their sacks of grain from the backs of the asses and placed them upon the ground. Then the servant, beginning with the sack of the oldest brother, searched each and every sack. At length he came to Benjamin's, and there the cup was found.

When the brothers, who had been watching all the while, saw this, they were filled with shame and

sorrow. They returned at once to Joseph and flung themselves upon the ground before him. "Why have you done this to me?" Joseph asked.

Juda spoke for the others and said, "What is there for us to say? God knows how wicked we have been and He is punishing us. We shall all stay and be your slaves."

"No, I will not let you do that," Joseph answered. "Only he who stole my cup shall be my slave."

Juda was sad indeed. "Hear me, my lord, and be not angry with me," he cried. "When we left Chanaan I promised our father that I would care for the boy and bring him safely home again. Our father is an old man and he loves Benjamin tenderly. If he sees that the boy is not with us when we return, his sorrow will surely kill him. Have pity, I beg of you, and let Benjamin go home with his brothers. Keep me as your slave in his place, for I could not return without him."

Finally Joseph could keep his secret no longer. He sent everyone out of the room except his brothers and, when he was alone with them, he began to weep so loud that all the people in the house heard him.

Then he said, "I am Joseph!"

The brothers were so frightened and surprised that they could not speak.

But Joseph spoke to them very kindly, saying, "I am Joseph, your brother, whom you sold into Egypt. Be not afraid. It was God's will that I should come to Egypt. He sent me here so that I could help you. It was God Who made me chief of the king's household and governor of Egypt. He helped me to see that enough food was stored so that Egypt would not suffer from the famine.

"Now hurry and go to our father and tell him to come to me. He and his sons and his grandsons and his sheep and herds shall dwell in Gessen near me. There are five more years of famine to come, and I shall feed my people during that time. Tell my father of my importance. Hurry and bring him to me."

The story of Joseph and his brothers came to the ears of the king and it made him very happy. He sent a message to the brothers, saying, "Bring back your father and your relatives and come to me. I will give you all the good things of Egypt. Take wagons out of Egypt to carry your wives and children and leave nothing behind in Chanaan. All the riches of Egypt shall be yours."

JACOB GOES TO EGYPT

The brothers did as they were commanded. Joseph told his servants to fill the wagons with food so that they would have enough to eat on the way. He sent many fine gifts to his father. To each of his brothers he gave a new robe. But to Benjamin he gave five robes and three hundred pieces of silver.

When Jacob's sons reached Chanaan they said to their father, "Joseph is still living and he is governor over all Egypt."

At first Jacob did not believe his sons. But when they showed him the wagons and the gifts that they had brought, he doubted their word no longer. He said, "Joseph my son is still alive! I will go and see him before I die!"

Soon Jacob set out for Egypt with his sons, their wives and their children. He took his flocks, his herds and all his possessions with him. On the way he stopped and offered sacrifice to God. That night, as he lay asleep, God spoke to him and said, "Do not be afraid to go down into Egypt, Jacob. For there I will make a great nation of you and your children."

Now, as they came near, Juda went on ahead of the others to tell Joseph that they were coming. As soon as Joseph heard this, he got into his chariot and rode out to meet his father and to welcome him. When he saw him, he threw his arms about his neck, kissed him and wept. And Jacob said, "Now I shall die in peace, for I have seen your face and know that you are still alive."

Joseph took Jacob before the king, and the king commanded him to give Jacob and his sons the best that was to be had in the land of Egypt. Jacob blessed the king who had been so kind to Joseph.

Joseph gave his father and his brothers the best land in Gessen for their home. He gave them charge over the king's cattle, and they lived in Gessen for seventeen years.

Jacob died in Gessen when he was very old. Before he died, he blessed his twelve sons and told them many things that would happen to them and their

families. To his son Juda, he told that his family and his heirs would rule over all his brothers' families and descendants.

Joseph and his brothers mourned the death of their father for seventy days. All the princes of the land of Egypt, all great men, and all the brothers of Joseph went to Chanaan to bury Jacob. There were many chariots and men on horseback. When they reached Chanaan, they mourned for Jacob seven days. Then they buried him with Abraham. After the funeral, Joseph and his brothers and the whole company went back to Egypt. There they stayed, and they grew in number and became prosperous.

SUGGESTIONS FOR STUDY

1. WHO AM I?

   a. I was Jacob's youngest son.
   b. I was Jacob's favorite son.
   c. I made Joseph the governor of my country.
   d. I coaxed my brothers to sell Joseph as a slave.
   e. I had Joseph put into prison.

2. ANSWER YES OR NO.

   a. The chief butler remembered his promise to Joseph.
   b. Joseph's brothers were jealous of him.
   c. God gave Joseph the power to explain dreams.
   d. Joseph's brothers recognized him when they met him in Egypt.
   e. God told Jacob that it was His will that Jacob take his whole family to live in Egypt.

3. FILL IN THE BLANKS WITH THESE WORDS.

   famine   beast   Juda   wise   baker

   a. Jacob thought that Joseph had been killed by a —————.
   b. Joseph explained the dreams of the ————— and chief butler while in prison.
   c. The ————— men of the kingdom could not tell the king what his dreams meant.
   d. The seven thin cows stood for seven years of —————.
   e. The family of ————— was the one that was to rule over the other descendants of Jacob.

4. DRAW A LINE UNDER THE CORRECT ANSWER.

   a. The king chose Joseph as (governor—prince) of all Egypt.
   b. When his brothers came to Egypt, Joseph wished to hear about his (father—mother).

c. Joseph wanted to learn whether his brothers (hated—feared) him as much as they did when they sold him to the merchants.

d. (Simeon—Ruben) was put into prison by Joseph.

e. Joseph insisted that his brothers bring back (Benjamin—Jacob) when they came again.

5. MATCH COLUMN I WITH COLUMN II.

a. Juda   ( ) had the servants put a silver cup in Benjamin's sack.

b. Jacob   ( ) favored Joseph.

c. God   ( ) begged Joseph not to keep Benjamin.

d. Joseph   ( ) did not go to Egypt until the third time.

e. The king   ( ) made Joseph head of his household.

6. HOW WELL CAN YOU THINK?

a. Joseph's brothers were very unkind to him. Yet he repaid them with kindness. How should we repay others when they are unkind to us?

b. In former times God sometimes taught men through dreams. Today we are taught by Christ through His Church. How does the Church teach us the truths of our religion?

7. DO YOU KNOW WHAT THESE WORDS MEAN?

misery	famine	gallows	sheaf
wrath	sprouted	devoured	plenty
shrunken	annoyed	harvest	stain

VII † MOSES, DELIVERER OF THE ISRAELITES

THE CHILD AMONG
THE REEDS

Joseph and his brothers lived in Egypt for many years. After they had died, their children and their children's children spread to all parts of the land. For a long time they lived peacefully and happily. They grew wealthy and increased in numbers. Wherever they went, they were spoken of as the "Children of Israel," or "Israelites," because Jacob, their grandfather, had sometimes been called Israel instead of Jacob, that being the name given him by the angel with whom he had wrestled.

Years passed and then a new king came to rule over Egypt. He saw the Children of Israel about him on every side. He said to the Egyptians, "The land will soon be filled with these strangers who have come to live among us. I fear that they will become greater and stronger than we are. Let us treat them harshly so that they cannot gain too much strength or power."

The Egyptians heard their king, and they too grew to dislike the Israelites. They made them their slaves and forced them to work at building roads and cities. They placed cruel masters over them who beat them.

But even though the Egyptians hated them and treated them cruelly, the Children of Israel grew stronger and stronger. The king, seeing this, became more frightened and he commanded that every baby boy born among the Israelites be thrown into the river. He said, "We must not let these babies grow up to be strong men who will fight against us."

At this time a baby boy was born to one of the Israelite women. The mother loved her baby dearly and made up her mind that she would not let the king's soldiers throw him into the river. She hid him in her house for three months. When she could no longer hide him, she made a basket of the tall grasses, or reeds, that grew along the river. She covered this basket with pitch so that water could not get into it. Then she placed the baby in it and hid it among the reeds that grew on the bank of the river near the palace of the king's daughter. She told Miriam, the baby's sister, to stand near and watch and see what would happen to the baby.

The baby had not been there very long when the king's daughter came down to the river to bathe.

Seeing the basket among the reeds she sent one of her maids to fetch it. When the maid opened it, the king's daughter saw in it the little baby and she knew that it was one of the Israelite babies. She pitied the baby, for it was crying, and she decided to save it.

Now Miriam saw everything that happened. She ran to the princess and said, "Shall I call an Israelite woman to care for the baby?"

The princess answered, "Yes," and the girl went at once and called her mother, who was also the mother of the little baby.

When the princess saw the baby's mother, she said to her, "Take this child and nurse it. I will pay you."

The mother took her baby and cared for him. When he was old enough so that he no longer needed her, she took him to the princess. The princess was overjoyed when she saw the boy, for he had grown to be a bright sturdy lad. She took him to live in the palace with her and she loved him as her own son. She said, "I will call the boy Moses, for I drew him out of the water." That is what Moses means.

Although Moses lived like a prince in the palace, he often thought of his own people and grew lonesome for them. When he was older, he liked to walk through the streets of the city where the Hebrew men were working. But sometimes he grew sad as he watched them, for they had to work very hard, digging and carrying heavy stones. They could never stop to rest, no matter how hot or tired they were.

One day, as Moses was walking along, he saw an Egyptian strike one of the Israelite workmen. This made Moses very angry and he in turn struck the Egyptian and killed him.

It was not long before the king heard what Moses had done and he made up his mind to put the young Israelite to death. But Moses fled from Egypt and went to live in a land called Madian.

It took him many days to reach Madian. Once, when near a town, he sat by a well to rest. As he was sitting there, the daughters of a man named Raguel, also called Jethro, came to draw water for their father's sheep. Just as they were about to fill the troughs with water, some other shepherds came and pushed them aside. When Moses saw this he drove these shepherds away. Then he stood by and helped the maidens care for their sheep.

When the daughters of Raguel went home, they told their father about Moses. He said, "Where is the man? Call him that we may make him welcome."

Moses went to Raguel's home and stayed there many days. He finally decided to go no farther. He made his home in Madian and cared for Raguel's flocks. He also married one of Raguel's daughters.

THE BURNING BUSH

After a long time the king, whose daughter had cared for Moses, died and a new king ruled over Egypt. This new king was not a good man. The Children of Israel feared him, for he treated them even more cruelly than they had been treated before. The Israelites begged God to save them.

God heard the cries of His people and He pitied them. He had never forgotten that He had promised to make them a great nation.

Moses had been away from Egypt all these years. He had lived in Madian caring for Raguel's flocks. He was very happy there with his wife and children. One day, while he was leading his sheep through the country, he came to Mount Horeb. There he saw a strange sight. Flames of fire were coming from a bush that was growing near by and, though the flames were burning fiercely, the bush was not burned up.

When Moses saw this he was filled with wonder. He gazed at the bush for a while and then he walked toward it to see why it did not burn up. As he did so, a voice said to him from the midst of it, "Moses, Moses."

Moses could see no one, but he answered, "Here I am."

Then the voice spoke again and said, "Do not come closer, but take off your shoes, for the place where you are standing is holy ground. I am the God of your father, the God of Abraham, the God of Isaac and the God of Jacob."

Moses hid his face, for he dared not look up. Then he heard God speaking once more and saying, "I have seen how unhappy My people are in Egypt and I have heard them cry out because their masters, the Egyptians, have treated them so harshly. And knowing their sorrows, I have come to free them and to lead them to a better land. I will send you to the king that you may bring the Children of Israel out of Egypt."

It made Moses very happy to think that God had chosen him to lead the Children of Israel out of Egypt, but yet he was afraid. He did not think that the king or the people would listen to him. So he said to God, "Alas! who am I that I should stand before the king and lead these people out of his land? They do not even know me. They will ask, 'Who are you, and who has sent you?'"

"Be not afraid," God answered, "I will be with you. And after you have led My people out of Egypt, you shall offer sacrifice to Me upon this mountain as a sign to them that it was I, Who sent you.

"Go, then, to Egypt and say to the Children of Israel, 'The Lord God of your fathers has seen your sorrows and He has decided to lead you into a land that is flowing with milk and honey.' When the people have heard this, they will listen to you. Then you and their leaders shall go together to the king and you shall say to him, 'The Lord God of the Hebrews has called us. We beg of you, let us go on a three days' journey into the desert that we may offer sacrifice to Him.' But the king will not listen to you and he will not let you go. Then I will stretch forth My hand and I will send misfortunes to him and his people. After that, he will let you go."

"But what shall I do if the Children of Israel will not listen to me or believe me?" Moses asked. "They may even say the Lord God has not appeared to me."

Then God asked, "What do you have in your hand?"

Moses answered, "It is a staff."

This staff was the one that Moses used when he led his sheep to pasture. God said to him, "Throw your staff on the ground."

Moses did as God commanded, and instantly the staff was turned into a serpent. Moses was frightened and he backed away from the serpent. But God said, "Put out your hand and take the serpent by the tail."

Moses did so, and at once the serpent was changed back into his staff.

God then said, "Put your hand inside your garment." Moses did as he was told and when he drew his hand out from his garment, it was covered with leprosy.

"Put your hand back into your garment, then take it out and look at it again," God then told him. Moses did so, and when he withdrew it, the leprosy was gone.

God said to him, "If the Children of Israel will not believe you when you speak to them, show them these two signs that I have shown to you. And if they still will not listen to your words, take water from the river and pour it upon the dry land. The water which you pour shall be turned into blood."

Moses bowed his head when he heard all these things which God had said. He knew that the Children of Israel would believe him when he showed them the wonderful signs, but he did not speak well and he feared that they would not understand him. So he said to God, "You know that I am not very good as a speaker."

God said to him, "Go and do not fear, for I will be with you and will teach you what to say."

Moses was still troubled and he begged God to send someone else in his place.

God was not pleased at this, but He said to Moses, "You have a brother named Aaron who speaks well. He is coming to meet you and when he sees you, he will be glad. Speak to him when he comes and tell him what I have told you. He shall speak to the people instead of you. But you shall guide him and tell him what to say."

Moses returned to his home at once. He told Raguel that he wished to return to Egypt, and Raguel replied, "Go, and may God be with you."

So Moses bade Raguel good-bye, and he and his wife and children set out for Egypt. He carried his staff in his hand. On the way he met Aaron, just as God had said he would. The two brothers were very happy to see each other and, as they traveled along together, Moses told Aaron what had happened.

When they came to Egypt, they called the Children of Israel together and Aaron gave them God's message. Then he showed them the wonderful signs. The people listened to every word that he spoke and when he told them that God had seen their suffering and had sent Moses to help them, their hearts were filled with joy. They fell down on their knees and thanked the Lord God of their Fathers.

MOSES AND AARON BEFORE THE KING

After Moses and Aaron had spoken to the Israelites, they went to the king of Egypt and said to him, "The Lord God of Israel has sent us to ask you to let His people go on a three days' journey into the desert to offer sacrifice to Him."

"Who is this Lord God of Israel of Whom you speak?" asked the king. "I do not know Him. Neither will I heed His words." Then he turned to his officials and told them to give the Children of Israel more work to do so that they would not have time to think of offering sacrifices to their God.

The officials did as the king ordered. And not only did they give the people more work to do, but they whipped them when the work was not finished.

When Moses saw how the people were treated, he called out to God and said, "Why did You send me to Egypt? Since I spoke to the king in Your name, the sorrows of the people have been greater than they were before. Why have You treated them so?"

God heard Moses and He said, "Now you shall see what I will do to the king. Do not be troubled, but go to My people and tell them that I have not forgotten them and that I will take care of them."

Moses went to the Children of Israel and told them all that God had said, but they would not listen to him. They were angry with him and they trusted him no longer.

God told Moses and Aaron to go before the king a second time and demand that he let the Children of Israel go out of Egypt. Moses and Aaron did as God commanded, and when the king heard their message, he said, "Let the God of the Israelites give me a sign if He wishes His people to leave my land." Moses then told Aaron to throw his staff on the ground before the king, and when he did this it became a serpent. Then the king called the magicians and wise men of his kingdom and they cast their staffs on the ground, and their staffs likewise became serpents. But Aaron's serpent ate up the serpents of the magicians.

The king was surprised when he saw this, but still he refused to let the Israelites leave his land.

Then God said to Moses, "Arise early in the morning and go with Aaron to the king. You will find the king walking along the bank of the river. Tell him that I have sent you, and ask him once more to let My people go."

Moses and Aaron arose early and went to meet the king, but again he would not listen to their plea. So Aaron touched the water of the river with his staff and at once the water was turned into blood. The fishes that lived in it died and there was no water in the land for the people to drink.

GOD PUNISHES THE EGYPTIANS

After seven days had passed, Moses and Aaron went again to the king and said to him, "The Lord God of Israel has again sent us. He says if you do not let His people go into the desert to offer sacrifice to Him, He will send frogs to cover the land." As had happened before, the king would not listen to them nor would he let the Hebrews leave the land. So once more Aaron stretched his staff over the river and

frogs came up and covered the whole country of Egypt. There were frogs in the houses and on the beds, in the ovens and on the food.

Then the king called Moses and Aaron to him and said to them, "Pray to your God and ask Him to take the frogs away from me and my people and I will let you and your people go to offer sacrifice to Him."

Moses prayed to God and God took the frogs away from the whole country. The only place where they remained was along the river. But the king was not an honest man. When he saw that the frogs had disappeared, he did not keep his word. Aaron then struck the dust with his staff and it was changed

into fleas. They rose like a cloud of dust and covered both men and beasts. And, although the people of his land suffered, the stubborn king would not consent to let the Children of Israel leave Egypt.

Next, God sent a great swarm of flies over Egypt. They spread through the land, and the houses of the Egyptians were filled with them. But they did not come into the section where the Hebrews lived.

This troubled the king and, calling Moses to him, he said, "If your God takes these flies away from Egypt, I will let His people go into the desert to offer sacrifice in His name."

God heard the prayer of Moses and He took away the flies from the land. But no sooner had He done so, than the king's heart grew hard again and he would not let the Children of Israel go.

Then God sent other plagues upon Egypt, one worse than the other. There was sickness and suffering everywhere. God did not spare the king or those who belonged to him. But still the king would not listen to Moses.

When God saw this, He spoke to Moses and said, "I will send one more plague upon the Egyptians and it shall be worse than all the others. When it has come, the king will know that My power is great and he will let My people go."

Moses warned the king of Egypt and told him all about the terrible plague that God was going to send upon his people. But the king was a foolish man and paid no attention to him.

Moses spoke to the Children of Israel and ordered each family to kill a young lamb and sprinkle the top and sides of the doorways of their houses with its blood. This lamb was then to be roasted. After that, it was to be eaten with wild lettuce, and bread which had been made without yeast.

Moses then told the Israelites that God would destroy the first-born of all the Egyptians. He said that those houses with blood on their doorposts would

be passed by, and none of the children inside would be harmed.

The Israelites did everything Moses commanded. That night, at midnight, there was great sorrow, for the oldest child in each house of the Egyptians died. Even the first-born of their animals died.

During the night the king arose and sent for Moses and Aaron and said to them, "Go out of Egypt."

The Israelites always celebrated this night as the Pasch, or Passover, for their houses were passed over, and their children left unharmed.

THE ISRAELITES LEAVE EGYPT

As soon as the Children of Israel heard that the king was willing to let them go out of Egypt, they gathered together their children, their flocks, their herds and all their possessions. Before they left on the journey, Moses divided them into companies. God Himself watched over them and guided them. He sent a column of cloud before them to show the way by day, and at night the column of cloud changed to a column of fire that lighted the darkness.

When the king heard that the Children of Israel had gone, he was sorry that he had let them go. He made up his mind to follow them and bring them

back again. So he called together the captains of his army and his soldiers and they set out in great chariots drawn by strong horses to overtake the Israelites.

Now, the Israelites had stopped to rest when they reached the shores of the Red Sea. While they were camping there, they saw the king and his army drawing near and they were filled with terror. The sea was in front of them and the Egyptians were behind them. They did not know what to do. So they cried out to Moses and asked him why he had taken them out of Egypt to die in the desert.

Moses comforted the people, saying, "Fear not, the Lord will care for you."

Then the column of cloud that had gone before the Children of Israel went behind them, and hid them from the Egyptians.

God then told Moses to stretch his hand over the waters. Moses did so and at once the waters rolled back and divided the sea. During the night a strong warm wind sprang up. It blew all night long and dried the path of land that was between the two walls of water. In the morning the Children of Israel marched through the sea on dry land. The Egyptians followed them, but when they were in the middle of the sea, God sent a storm that upset their chariots and killed their horses. This frightened the soldiers of the king and they tried to turn back. They said, "The God of the Hebrews is fighting for them against us."

After the Israelites had passed through the sea and were safe on the other shore, Moses, at God's command, stretched forth his hand again and the waters came together. The Egyptians who were trying to escape were drowned and their bodies floated upon the water.

When the Israelites saw this, they knew that God had protected them. They joined with Moses and sang a hymn of praise to God to show how grateful they were.

SUGGESTIONS FOR STUDY

1. FILL IN THE BLANKS WITH THESE WORDS.

plagues   Aaron   Israelites   Horeb   Red Sea

a. The _____ were also called the Children of Israel.
b. Moses saw the burning bush on Mount _____.
c. _____ was Moses' brother.
d. God sent _____ on Egypt.
e. God helped the Israelites cross the _____ safely.

2. DRAW A LINE UNDER THE CORRECT ANSWER.

a. The first-born of the Egyptians were (saved—killed).
b. Moses was born of (Egyptian—Jewish) parents.
c. God told (Moses—Aaron) to lead His people out of Egypt.
d. The (Israelites—Egyptians) were drowned in the Red Sea.
e. Moses married and settled in (Madian—Mount Horeb).

3. WHO AM I?

a. I helped Moses lead the Israelites out of Egypt.
b. I was Moses' sister.
c. I let my daughter marry Moses.
d. I spoke to Moses from the Burning Bush.

4. HOW WELL CAN YOU THINK?

a. The blood of a lamb sprinkled on their doorposts saved the first-born of the Israelites. We, too, are saved by the Precious Blood of the Lamb of God. In what sacrament do we receive this Precious Blood? Why should we receive this sacrament often?
b. God gave Moses the power to work certain signs in order to show the Israelites that God had sent him to save them from the Egyptians. What signs has God given His Church to prove that He is always with us?

c. Moses was a poor speaker and God sent his brother, Aaron, to speak for him. How can we speak for God in our daily life?

5. ANSWER YES OR NO.
   a. The Egyptians feared the Israelites.
   b. God sent plagues to punish the Egyptians.
   c. The king of Egypt was an honest man.
   d. Moses' mother was not frightened that her baby might be killed.
   e. As a young man, Moses lived like a prince.

6. CAN YOU USE THESE WORDS IN SENTENCES?

frightened	plagues	yeast
reeds	troughs	doorpost
swarm	staff	terror

VIII † MOSES, THE GREAT LEADER

GOD CARES FOR
THE ISRAELITES
After the Israelites had passed through the Red Sea, they came into a desert. They marched for three days and could not find any water. Finally they came to a place named Mara. There they found water, but it was so bitter that they could not drink it. They began to be sorry that they had left Egypt. They murmured against Moses saying, "What shall we drink?"

When this happened, Moses went and prayed to the Lord. The Lord heard his prayer and showed him a piece of wood. When Moses cast the wood into the bitter waters of the spring, the water became sweet.

After the Israelites had rested there a while, they again went on their way. Soon the food which they had brought with them was gone and they began to complain to Moses, asking him why he had brought them into the desert to die of hunger.

God heard their murmurs and He spoke to Moses and said, "Behold, I have heard the murmuring of My people and in order that they may know that I am their God and have not forgotten them, I will rain down bread from heaven and send them meat to eat."

That evening a large number of quail flew into the camp. These were easily caught and eaten. In the morning the Israelites noticed that the ground around the camp was covered with small, white flakes. There were so many of these that the ground looked as if it were covered with frost.

When the Israelites saw this, they cried out, "What is this?" This bread is called manna. Moses told them that they were to gather each day only enough for that day. After the sun grew hot, the manna that was left on the earth melted. On the sixth day they were to gather enough for two days, for on the seventh day, the Sabbath, the manna did not fall.

As the Israelites wandered on through the desert, they came to a camping place where there was no water. Once again they were thirsty and they called out to Moses, saying, "Give us water that we may drink, or we shall die of thirst."

Moses prayed to God once more. He said, "What shall I do? My people are angry with me and I fear they will kill me."

Then the Lord told Moses to take his rod and strike a rock on the side of Mount Horeb. Moses did as God commanded and, when he struck the rock, water came out of it and all the people had enough to drink.

While the Israelites were in the desert, a tribe of people called the Amalecites battled with them. Moses sent a brave man named Josue with some of the men of Israel to drive this enemy away. When Josue left for battle, Moses, Aaron and Hur went to the top of a mount near by and Moses lifted up his hands and prayed. As long as his hands were raised, all went well with Josue and his men. But when Moses became tired and lowered his arms, the battle went against the Israelites. Seeing this, Aaron and Hur held up the arms of their leader until at sunset the Children of Israel conquered the Amalecites and put them to flight.

THE TEN COMMANDMENTS

In the third month after the Children of Israel had left Egypt, they came into the desert around Mount Sinai, or Horeb, and camped near the mountain.

God called Moses to the top of the mountain and spoke to him. He told Moses to prepare the people during the two following days, for on the third day He would appear to them.

On the third day it thundered and lightning flashed, and a thick cloud covered the mountain. A trumpet sounded. The people were very much afraid. Moses led them from the camp to the foot of the mountain. Smoke rose from the mountain as from a furnace, and the sound of the trumpet grew louder and louder.

Then the Lord spoke:

"I am the Lord thy God. Thou shalt not have strange gods before Me.

"Thou shalt not take the name of the Lord thy God in vain.

"Remember thou keep holy the Sabbath Day.

"Honor thy father and thy mother.

"Thou shalt not kill.

"Thou shalt not commit adultery.

"Thou shalt not steal.

"Thou shalt not bear false witness against thy neighbor.

"Thou shalt not covet thy neighbor's wife.

"Thou shalt not covet thy neighbor's goods."

When the people saw the thunder and lightning, and heard the trumpet blast, they cried out to Moses, "Let not the Lord speak to us, or we shall die."

Moses answered, "Fear not. God has shown Himself to you like this so that the fear of Him might keep you from sin."

Then Moses went up to the dark cloud which covered the mountain. God was in this cloud. He spoke to Moses and gave him many laws which the Children of Israel were to obey.

God also told Moses that He had chosen the Israelites as His own special people. That is why they are called the Chosen People. He made a covenant with them. They were to love and obey Him; He would take special care of them.

After he had heard all these things, Moses came down from the cloud and told the people what God had said.

Soon after this, Moses left Aaron and Hur in charge of the Israelites while he again went up the mountain to speak to God. He stayed there for forty days and forty nights.

After Moses had been up in the mountain for a long while, the people came to Aaron and said, "Make gods for us that may go before us and lead us. We know not what has happened to Moses."

Aaron said to the people, "Bring the golden earrings of your wives and children to me."

When this jewelry had been brought to Aaron, he melted the gold and made it into a golden calf. He gave this calf to the people, and they worshiped it and offered sacrifices to it.

Then the Lord spoke to Moses and said, "Go down to the people whom you brought out of Egypt, for they have sinned. They have made a golden calf and have been adoring it. Because they have been so wicked I will destroy them."

But Moses begged God not to destroy the Israelites. God listened to his prayer and consented to spare them.

As Moses came down from the mountain, he carried in his hands two tables of stone upon which God Himself had written the Ten Commandments. When he came nearer the camp of the Israelites, he saw the people worshiping the golden calf. This made him so angry that he threw the tables of stone upon the ground and broke them. Then he went up to the golden calf and pulled it down, burnt it and beat it into powder.

After this, Moses again went up into the mountain and prayed for the people. He asked God to forgive them. God did forgive them, and told Moses to lead them on toward the Promised Land.

Some time after Moses had returned to his people, God again spoke to him and told him to make two new tables of stone. Upon these tables God wrote the Ten Commandments once more.

God had told Moses that the people were to make certain things to be used when they worshiped Him.

One of the things they were to make was a beautiful box of precious wood, lined and overlaid with gold. They were to make two angels which were to be placed on the cover of the box. In it they were to place the Commandments given by God. This box was called the Ark of the Commandments, or the Ark of the Covenant.

They were also to make a large tent of fine linen, embroidered in violet, purple and scarlet. This tent was called the Tabernacle, and in it they were to place the Ark of the Covenant.

The Israelites made these things as God had commanded. They carried them everywhere they went.

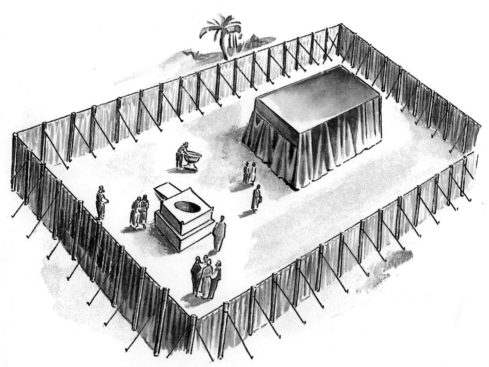

After the Children of Israel had camped near Mount Sinai, or Herob, for a year, Moses led them toward the Promised Land. One day God spoke to Moses, saying, "Send men to see the Land of Chanaan which I have promised to give to the Children of Israel."

The Children of Israel were divided into twelve companies. Moses chose one man from each company. He said to them, "Go and see what sort of land it is. Find out how many people live there and what they are like. Find out if the land is good or bad, and if there are trees and fruit. If you find any fruit, bring some back to us."

The scouts set out for the Land of Chanaan. After forty days they returned to the Israelite camp with a bunch of grapes so large that it took two men to carry it. They also brought back other fruit which they had gathered. The scouts then told of the land and the people they had seen. They said, "The land is very rich, as you can see from the size of these grapes. But it will be dangerous for us to go into it, for the people living there are very strong and the cities have high walls around them."

When the Israelites heard this, they were frightened and began to wish that they had died in the desert.

Some of them wanted to choose a captain who would lead them back to Egypt. They were very angry with Moses and Aaron. They would not listen to them any more.

But among the scouts who had been sent into the Promised Land were two good men, Josue and Caleb. They said to the people, "The land is very good, and if it is God's will, He will lead us into it. Do not be afraid of the people who live there. God is with us, and He will help us to conquer them."

But the people would not listen to Josue and Caleb. They even tried to stone them.

Then God became very angry with the Israelites. He told Moses that He would strike them with a terrible sickness and destroy them. But again Moses prayed to God and asked Him to have patience with the people and to forgive them. God heard the prayer of Moses and forgave the people.

It was very wrong for the Children of Israel to wish to go back to Egypt. It showed that they did not trust God and did not wish to obey Him. So God said to Moses and Aaron, "How long will this wicked people murmur against me? I have heard their complaints and I am not pleased. All those who are twenty years old and over and who have murmured against Me shall not enter the Promised Land. Of these, only

Caleb and Josue shall enter it. The Children of Israel shall wander in the desert for forty years."

In this way the Israelites were punished for their disobedience.

THE ISRAELITES IN THE DESERT

The Israelites wandered about in the desert; they could find no water and no fruit and they became dissatisfied and murmured against Moses and Aaron. When Moses and Aaron heard this, they went into the Tabernacle, cast themselves on the ground and prayed to God, saying, "O Lord, hear the cry of the people, and open to them a fountain of water, that they may be satisfied. Give them water to drink that they may stop their murmuring."

Then God told Moses to take his rod and strike a rock. God said that water should come forth from it. Moses gathered the people together in front of the rock and struck it twice, and the water gushed forth so that there was plenty for all the people and their cattle to drink.

As Moses struck the rock, he thought of how wicked the Children of Israel had been. He thought that maybe God would not give them water this time. Moses doubted God's mercy toward the people, and so God said that He would not permit Moses to lead them into the Promised Land.

Some time later the people were again without water and again they murmured against Moses, saying: "Why did you bring us out of Egypt? We shall die in the desert. We have no water and are tired of eating manna."

When God heard this, He sent serpents among the people to bite them. These serpents had a sting which was like fire. Many of the people suffered terribly from the stings. Some of the people even died. The rest ran to Moses and begged him to take away the serpents.

Moses prayed to God for the people, and God said

to him, "Make a serpent of bronze and set it up on a pole. All who look at it shall live."

Moses did as God commanded, and made the serpent and set it up on a pole. Those who were bitten looked up at the bronze serpent and were cured at once.

THE DEATH OF MOSES

After forty years of wandering in the desert, Moses called the Children of Israel together and blessed them. He appointed Josue their leader, as God had commanded. Then he went up into a high mountain called Mount Nebo. From the top of this mountain God showed him the Land of Chanaan and said to him, "This is the land which I will give to the people. You have seen it with your eyes, but you shall not enter it."

When Moses died, the Children of Israel mourned for thirty days. After their mourning was over, Josue took command of the people.

One morning before daylight, the Israelites broke camp and marched until they came to the river Jordan. They stayed there three days. On the third day the priests took the Ark of the Covenant and went to the river. As soon as their feet touched the Jordan, the waters were rolled back, leaving a path of dry land in the bottom of the river. Then the Israelites marched along this path. When the priests with the Ark of the Covenant were halfway across, they stood still and waited until all the people had passed over. Then they followed after them. When the priests reached the other shore, the waters came together. At last the Israelites had reached the Promised Land, the country promised by God to their fathers.

SUGGESTIONS FOR STUDY

1. DRAW A LINE UNDER THE CORRECT ANSWERS.

   a. Moses told the Israelites to gather up only enough manna for one (week—day).
   b. God gave Moses the Ten Commandments on Mount (Carmel—Sinai).
   c. Another name for Mount Sinai is Mount (Olivet—Horeb).
   d. The people looked at the (golden calf—bronze serpent) to be cured.
   e. Aaron and Hur held up the arms of (Moses—Josue).

2. FILL IN THE BLANKS WITH THESE WORDS.

   Ark of the Covenant   manna   Ten Commandments
   forgive   worshiping

   a. Moses often asked God to ——————— the Israelites.
   b. The Israelites were fed with ——————— in the desert.
   c. God gave the Israelites the ———————.
   d. The people sinned by ——————— the golden calf.
   e. God commanded the Israelites to make the ———————.

3. MATCH COLUMN I WITH COLUMN II.

  a. large tent   ( ) Josue
  b. Land of Chanaan   ( ) Tabernacle
  c. led the Israelites into the ( ) Amalecites
     Promised Land
  d. fought the Israelites   ( ) Ten Commandments
  e. written on stone   ( ) Promised Land

4. WHO AM I?

  a. I told the Israelites to bring their gold to me so that I could make the golden calf.
  b. I entered the Promised Land with Josue.
  c. I doubted God's mercy toward the people.
  d. Aaron and I held up Moses' arms during the battle with the Amalecites.
  e. I fought and drove off the Amalecites.

5. HOW WELL CAN YOU THINK?

  a. All the bitten people who looked at the bronze serpent set on the pole were cured. Christ was also raised up on the cross. How did Christ save us from our spiritual ills?
  b. God gave Moses the Ten Commandments. Who must keep them? Why should we keep them?
  c. The Israelites were fed with manna in the desert. God also feeds us with Bread from heaven. What is this Bread? How can we receive it?

6. DO YOU KNOW WHAT THESE WORDS MEAN?

murmur	manna	battle
tabernacle	doubt	wander
melted	ills	spiritual

IX † GREAT SOLDIERS OF ISRAEL

After the Israelites had crossed the Jordan, they were in Chanaan, the Promised Land. Jacob had lived in Chanaan with his sons before they went into Egypt, and his twelve sons were the forefathers of the Israelites. That is why the Israelites were divided into twelve great companies, or tribes. Each tribe was named after one of the sons of Jacob. But the tribe of Joseph was divided into two tribes, those of his sons Ephraim and Manasses. The principal tribe was the tribe of Juda. Our Savior came from this tribe.

Josue gave each of the tribes a part of the Promised Land in which to live. The tribe of Levi, since they were priests, did not receive any land, but lived at various places among the other tribes.

Josue told the people of Israel that God wanted them to conquer the people of Chanaan because they worshiped false gods. But after Josue's death the Israelites did not do as God commanded them, for, instead of conquering the Chanaanites, they made peace with them. Some of the Israelites even married people of Chanaan. Those who did so soon forgot God and began to worship idols.

GEDEON LEADS ISRAEL TO VICTORY

God punished the Israelites by allowing their enemies to send armies against them. But He did not allow these armies to destroy the Israelites, for He raised up brave men to lead them in battle and rule over them. These men were called Judges.

The Judges ruled Israel for a very long time, and during that time there were sixteen of them. One of the most famous of these was a man named Gedeon. At the time he lived, a tribe of people called Madianites were fighting against the Israelites.

One day Gedeon was threshing wheat, when an angel appeared to him and said, "The Lord is with you, O bravest of men. Go in your strength and free Israel from the Madianites."

That night Gedeon called ten of his servants and they went into Madian and destroyed the altar of the god Baal. Baal was a false god of the Madianites.

Soon the Madianites gathered together a large army and marched against the Israelites. Gedeon prayed to God, saying, "If I am the one who is to save Israel, show me a sign, and let this be the sign: I shall put a fleece of wool on the ground. If tomorrow morning there be dew on the fleece, but the ground around it be dry, I shall know that You want me to save Israel from the Madianites."

Early in the morning before sunrise, Gedeon went out to look at the fleece. It was so wet that he wrung it with his hands and filled a whole dish with the dew. Yet the ground all around it was dry.

Again Gedeon prayed to God, saying, "Be not angry with me if I try once more to find a sign in the fleece. This time, let the fleece be dry and all the ground around wet with dew."

God did as Gedeon asked. The next morning the fleece was dry, and the ground all around was wet with dew. Then Gedeon knew that God wanted him to save Israel from the Madianites.

He selected three hundred men from the Israelite army and took them to fight the Madianites. These three hundred men he divided into three companies. To each man he gave a trumpet and an empty pitcher. He commanded them to put a lamp into each pitcher. He said, "Do whatever you see me do."

At midnight they all crept into the Madianite camp.
Then Gedeon blew his trumpet. At once the three
hundred men with him did the same. They broke
their pitchers open and held up their lamps and they
all shouted, "The sword of the Lord and Gedeon!"

The Madianites were so frightened and confused by
this noise that they began to kill one another. The
Israelites kept on blowing their trumpets, and the
Madianites began to run away.

Gedeon won many other victories for the Israelites,
and they loved him so much that they asked him to be
their king. But he said, "I will not be your king. The
Lord is your King, and He rules over you."

SUGGESTIONS FOR STUDY

1. WHO AM I?

   a. I gave each of the tribes a part of the Promised Land.
   b. I was a Judge who won many victories for the Israelites.
   c. My tribe was divided into two tribes.
   d. Our Savior came from my tribe.
   e. The members of my tribe were priests.

2. FILL IN THE BLANKS WITH THESE WORDS.

   conquer   Judges   Baal   Israelites   peace

   a. The —————— were brave men who led the Israelites in battle and ruled over them.
   b. Jacob's twelve sons were the forefathers of the ——————.
   c. Josue told the people that God wanted them to —————— the people of Chanaan.
   d. After Josue's death, the Israelites made —————— with the Chanaanites.
   e. —————— was a false god.

3. HOW WELL CAN YOU THINK?

   a. Gedeon asked God for two signs so that he would be sure to know what God wanted him to do. How can we know what God wants us to do?
   b. Gedeon was a just and able man who served God well. How can you serve God well in your daily life?

4. CAN YOU USE THESE WORDS IN SENTENCES?

forefathers	tribe	principal
famous	fleece	selected
Judge	companies	disobedience

X † GREAT RULERS OF ISRAEL

GOD APPOINTS SAMUEL
TO RULE   Another one of the
Judges was named Samuel. His father's name was
Elcana and his mother's name was Anna. God sent
Samuel to Anna in answer to her prayer. She was
growing old and had no children. She promised God
that if He would send her a son, she would give him
to the Lord all the days of his life.

While Samuel was still a child, she took him to the
house of the Lord and left him with Heli the priest.
Heli taught Samuel how to serve the priests and gave
him tasks to do. He was a good little boy.

Now, Samuel slept near Heli, in the part of the
house of the Lord where the Ark was kept. One night
he heard a voice calling him, saying, "Samuel."

Samuel awoke and answered, "Here I am."

There was no one in the room, so he ran to Heli
and said, "Here I am, for you called me."

But Heli said, "I did not call you. Go back and go to sleep." So Samuel went back and went to sleep.

A little while later, he again heard a voice calling, "Samuel." He arose and went at once to Heli and said, "Here I am, for you called me."

Heli said, "I did not call you, my son. Go back to sleep." Again Samuel went back and fell asleep.

The voice called the third time, "Samuel." He arose and went to Heli and said, "Here I am, for you called me." Then Heli knew that it was the Lord Himself Who was calling Samuel, and he said to him, "Go and sleep, and if the voice calls again say: 'Speak, Lord; your servant hears you.'" So Samuel again went back and fell asleep.

Again the voice called, "Samuel, Samuel." The boy said, "Speak, Lord; your servant hears you." Then God told Samuel that He was going to punish Heli and his sons because the sons of Heli were very wicked and their father did not correct them.

Samuel slept until morning and then got up and opened the doors of the house of God, for that was one of his tasks. He was afraid to tell Heli what God had said. But Heli called him and asked him. Then Samuel told Heli what God had said.

A short time after this, Heli's sons were killed in battle, and the Ark of the Covenant was captured.

When Heli heard the news, he fell from the stool upon which he was sitting and broke his neck and died.

When Samuel grew up, he became a Judge of Israel. He prayed for the people when they were wicked, and God heard his prayer and forgave them.

When Samuel was an old man, he appointed his sons to be Judges over Israel, but they were wicked men and the people did not like them.

The time came when the Israelites wanted a king like other nations, and they asked Samuel to find one for them.

SAUL BECOMES FIRST KING OF ISRAEL

Samuel prayed to the Lord and told Him that the people wanted a king.

God heard Samuel's prayer and told him that He would appoint a king over all His chosen people.

God said that He would send a man of His choice to Samuel. He said that Samuel would know this man because He would tell Samuel when the man was to come.

The day before God's chosen man was to come, God warned Samuel. The man, Saul, came, and Samuel made

a great feast. Then he anointed Saul with oil as a sign
that God had chosen Saul to be king.

As Samuel anointed Saul he said to him, "Behold, the
Lord has appointed you ruler."

When the Israelites saw Saul, the man whom God
had chosen to be their first king, they were happy
indeed. Saul was strong and handsome. He stood head
and shoulders taller than any of the men of Israel. The
Israelites were sure that he would be good to them and
would protect them against their enemies.

At first all went well. Whenever Saul led the men
of Israel to battle, God was with them and they won
many victories. After a while, however, Saul grew

proud and disobeyed God. Then God ordered Samuel to tell Saul that he could no longer rule over His people. This made Saul very unhappy, and for long hours he would sit looking so cross and gloomy that all who saw him feared him. One day when he was sad and troubled, his servants sent for a young shepherd boy named David. David played the harp beautifully, and the servants thought his music would cheer their master.

Now, David was a handsome, brave young boy who loved God with all his heart. At God's command, Samuel had anointed the lad with oil. Saul did not know this. Neither did he know that David was to become king some day in his place. When he saw the boy, he grew to love him. David's life at the court of the king was a happy one. He and Jonathan, Saul's young son, grew to be fast friends.

The Children of Israel had many enemies, but the worst of these were the Philistines, with whom they were always fighting. A new war had now broken out between the Philistines and the Israelites. The Philistines had placed their camp on one mountain and the Israelites had placed theirs on another directly facing them. Only a narrow valley lay between them.

The Philistines had in their army a giant named Goliath. He wore a helmet of brass and was clothed in a coat of strong armor. His spear was so long and heavy that few men could lift it. Day after day, he came out of his tent, strode up and down the valley and called out in a loud voice to the army of Israel, "Choose one man and let him come down to fight me hand to hand. If he kills me, we will be servants of Israel, but if I kill him, you shall be our servants."

When Saul and his men heard these words, they were frightened. They knew that there was no man in their army strong enough to fight against Goliath. Every morning and every evening, for forty days, the giant came down into the valley but no one went to meet him.

One day David came into the camp of the Israelites to bring food to his brothers, who were fighting in the army of Saul. As he stood talking to them, Goliath again came down into the valley. When David heard what the giant said, he was very angry. He asked, "Who is this Philistine who dares to defy the army of God? I will go and fight him."

But King Saul said, "You are not able to fight against this giant, David. You are but a boy. This man has been a soldier since his youth."

David answered Saul, saying, "I cared for my father's sheep and killed a lion and a bear when they tried to steal a lamb from the flock. I will also kill this Philistine who laughs at the army of God. And do you not think that God will protect me from him just as He protected me from the paw of the lion and the paw of the bear?"

Saul said to David, "Go, and the Lord be with you."

Then Saul put a helmet of brass upon David's head and armed him with a coat of mail.

When David put on the armor and hung the sword at his side he could not walk, for he was not used to wearing such things. He took them off and, taking his staff, he went down to the brook and picked out five smooth stones. He placed them in a shepherd's bag which he carried with him. Then, taking his sling in

his hand, he went down into the valley to meet Goliath.

When the giant was close to David and saw that he was only a boy, he was very angry. "Am I a dog that you come against me with a staff?" he asked.

David answered, "You come to me with a sword and a shield and a spear. I come to you in the name of God. This day God will give you into my hands." Then David put a stone into his sling and threw it at Goliath. The stone struck the giant on the forehead and he fell to the earth. David had no sword of his own, so he took Goliath's and cut off his head.

When the Philistines saw David kill Goliath they were frightened and ran away.

When David grew older he was made King of Israel. He was a very good king, and during his reign he made the city of Jerusalem Israel's capital.

David was not only a great king; he was also a poet. He wrote beautiful poems called Psalms. Some of these Psalms are hymns of praise and thanksgiving to God and others tell of David's sorrow for his sins. David sometimes sinned grievously, but he was always sorry and tried to do better afterwards.

God loved David and He made a covenant with him that the Redeemer should descend from him.

When David died, his son Solomon became king. At the beginning of his reign Solomon asked God to make him wise. God answered his prayer.

Solomon built the great Temple at Jerusalem and made the Kingdom of Israel greater than ever. Solomon was the wisest king Israel ever had.

After Solomon died, his son, Roboam, became king. When the people found out that Roboam was going to be a harsh king, ten of the tribes revolted against him while two remained faithful. In this way the Jewish people became divided into the two kingdoms of Juda and Israel. Roboam ruled the Kingdom of Juda, and a man named Jeroboam ruled Israel.

SUGGESTIONS FOR STUDY

1. UNDERLINE THE CORRECT ANSWER.

   a. Samuel was a (king—judge—prophet).
   b. Psalms are (stories—lessons—poems).
   c. The Ark of the Covenant was (captured—destroyed—blessed).
   d. Samuel anointed Saul to be a (soldier—king—priest).
   e. David killed (Goliath—Saul—Heli).

2. ANSWER YES OR NO.

   a. God made a covenant with David.
   b. The sons of Heli were holy men.
   c. The Philistines were friends of the Israelites.
   d. David built the Temple at Jerusalem.
   e. Solomon made the Kingdom of Israel greater than ever.

3. WHO AM I?

   a. Samuel anointed me the first king of Israel.
   b. David and I became fast friends.
   c. God promised that the Redeemer would descend from me.
   d. I was the son of David and the wisest king.
   e. God called me four times during the night before I answered Him.

4. FILL IN THE BLANKS WITH THESE WORDS.

   unhappy   Heli   king   son   punished

   a. Anna promised she would give her _____ to the Lord.
   b. Samuel thought _____ called him.
   c. Heli and his sons were to be _____.
   d. The Israelites wanted a _____ like other nations.
   e. Because Saul could no longer rule over his people he became very _____.

5. HOW WELL CAN YOU THINK?

  a. Samuel, hearing a voice said, "Here I am. Speak, Lord; your servant hears you." How can you imitate Samuel when you are told to do something?

  b. David was not afraid to fight Goliath because he knew that God would protect him. Tell some ways in which God protects you.

  c. Saul, at first, was a good king and God was pleased with him. But he grew proud and disobedient. Can we be pleasing to God if we disobey or become proud? How can we be pleasing to God?

  d. Roboam was a harsh king and the people revolted against him. If we are unkind and harsh to our companions we hurt them and displease God. How does God want us to act toward our companions?

6. DO YOU KNOW WHAT THESE WORDS MEAN?

captured	proud	harsh
anoint	defy	psalms
cross	descend	gloomy

XI † GREAT PROPHETS

GOD WATCHES OVER HIS PROPHETS God was very kind to the Israelites, but they were sometimes very ungrateful, for they often adored false gods and committed many other sins. But God loved them. They were His chosen people. He loved them so much that He sent them holy men called Prophets. These men brought God's message to the people. They called the people back to God when they had sinned.

The prophets also foretold the coming of the Redeemer, for God did not want the people to forget that a Redeemer was to come to save them. God sent many of these holy men to the Israelites before Christ came on earth. Two of the most famous of them were Jeremias and Isaias. They foretold many events in the life of our Lord.

One of the great prophets was named Elias. He lived during the reign of King Achab. This king had married a pagan wife and, to please her, he built a temple to the false god Baal and adored him.

God sent Elias to the king. Elias told Achab that God would not send any rain to the kingdom for three years as a punishment for the king's sins. It happened as Elias had foretold. There was no rain, and soon the people did not have enough to eat or drink.

Elias, too, became very hungry and thirsty at this time, so God told him to go to a brook which was near the river Jordan. There a raven brought him bread and meat both in the morning and in the evening, and there was water in the brook for him to drink. But after a while this brook also dried up.

Then God told Elias to go to a town called Sarephta, where a widow would feed him. Elias did as God bade him and went to the town. When he arrived there, he saw the widow and he called her and said, "Give me a little water in a vessel that I may drink." And then, as she was going to get it, he called, "And bring me also a morsel of bread."

She told Elias that she had no bread, but only a handful of meal and a little oil.

Elias told her to go and make a little cake of the meal for him. He said that as long as the drought lasted, the meal and the oil would not grow less. The woman did as Elias told her, and the oil and the meal lasted until the drought was over, even though she baked a hearth cake every day for Elias, herself and her son.

ELIAS AND THE PROPHETS OF BAAL

In the third year of the drought, Elias went to King Achab again, and told him that the drought was sent because he worshiped Baal. The prophet said to Achab, "Call all the people together and send for the four hundred and fifty prophets of Baal. We shall show the people who the true God is."

When they were gathered on the Mount of Carmel, Elias said to the people, "I am the only prophet of God who is here, but there are four hundred and fifty prophets of Baal. Let the prophets of Baal take a bullock and cut it in pieces and lay it on an altar. There is to be no fire under it. I will also take a bullock and cut it in pieces and lay it on an altar without any fire. Then let the prophets of Baal call upon their god and I will call upon mine. The god that shall answer by setting the wood on fire is the true God."

All the people agreed that this was a good plan.

The prophets of Baal took their bullock and cut it in pieces. They placed it upon wood but put no fire under it. Then the prophets called upon Baal from morning until noon, saying, "O Baal, hear us." But there was no answer.

At noon Elias was tired of waiting and started to make fun of them. He said, "Cry louder. Perhaps Baal is talking to someone, or maybe he is on a journey, or asleep."

The prophets of Baal cried louder, but Baal did not answer.

Then Elias said to the people, "Come now to me." When the people had gathered round him, he built an altar of stones and dug a trench around it. He laid wood on the altar and cut a bullock in pieces and laid it upon the wood. After this, he had men pour water

over the altar and the bullock until it ran over and filled the trench. When this was done, he prayed to God, saying, "O God, show this day that You are the God of Israel, and that I am Your servant. Hear me, O Lord, hear me."

Immediately, God sent down fire from heaven. It burned up the bullock and the wood, and the stones and the dust. It even dried up the water in the trench.

When the people saw this, they cried. "The Lord is God. The Lord is God."

In a little while the wind began to blow and the rain fell. The rain came harder and harder. It was the first rain that had fallen in Israel in three years.

Elias preached to the people of Israel. He told them when they were doing wrong and that they should be sorry for their sins. He worked many miracles. One day, after many years of preaching, a chariot of fire, drawn by fiery horses, came down and took him up to Heaven.

SUGGESTIONS FOR STUDY

1. FILL IN THE BLANKS WITH THESE WORDS.

sorry   Jeremias   prophets   raven   chariot

a. The _____ were holy men sent by God with a message for the people.

b. Isaias and _____ foretold many events in the life of Our Lord.

c. A _____ brought Elias meat and bread.

d. Elias told the people that they should be _____ for their sins.

e. Elias was taken up to heaven in a _____ of fire.

2. MATCH COLUMN I WITH COLUMN II.

a. The Redeemer   ( ) was kind to the Israelites.
b. Achab   ( ) fed Elias for a long time.
c. The Israelites   ( ) was to come to save the Israelites.
d. A widow   ( ) was a king who adored Baal.
e. God   ( ) were sometimes ungrateful.

3. ANSWER YES OR NO.

a. Did Elias say that God was going to send a famine?
b. Did God send Elias to warn the king?
c. Did God send fire for Elias' sacrifice?
d. Did God send rain after Elias' sacrifice?
e. Did Elias preach to the people of Israel for a short time?

4. DRAW A LINE UNDER THE CORRECT ANSWER.

a. Elias was a (prophet—judge).
b. Elias foretold that God would send no rain for (four—three) years.
c. The drought was a punishment for the (people's—king's) sins.

1. The widow's meal and oil did not grow less even though she made a cake for her family and (Elias—Achab) every day.
e. Elias was the prophet of (God—Baal).

5. HOW WELL CAN YOU THINK?

a. God was displeased with Achab and the Israelites because they worshiped the false god Baal. Which of God's commandments did they break in doing this? Tell how this commandment is sometimes broken by people nowadays?
b. God looked after his prophet Elias and he did not want for food. Elias put all his trust in God. How can we imitate him?

6. CAN YOU USE THESE WORDS IN SENTENCES?

prophet	bullock	drought
foretold	moral	trench
chariot	reign	vessel

XII † TOBIAS
AND
HIS SON

A MAN WHO LOVED GOD
AND NEIGHBOR

One time when the Israelites were very wicked, God allowed the Assyrians to fight them. The Assyrians were a mighty nation and had a very fine army, so it was easy for them to conquer the Israelites. They captured many of them and took them back to Assyria.

A story is told about one of these men called Tobias, who loved God and kept the Commandments. He was also very kind to his fellow Israelites, and tried to help them in every way.

Now, the Assyrian king was cruel to the Israelites and he had many of them put to death. When his soldiers would kill a man, they often left his body lying in the street and did not bury it.

In the night Tobias used to go through the streets looking for the bodies of Israelites. When he found them he would bury them.

Then, someone told the king that Tobias was burying the dead, and the king ordered his soldiers to kill Tobias. Tobias had to flee from the city and hide himself. When this wicked king was killed by his own sons, a new king succeeded him and he was kinder to the Jews. Tobias heard this and returned to the city from which he had fled.

When he came back, Tobias continued to work very hard for the other Israelites. One day, tired out, he lay down near a wall to sleep. While he was sleeping, some dirt from a swallow's nest fell into his eyes and made him blind. God sent him this injury as a test of his faith and patience.

A JOURNEY FAR FROM HOME

Because of his blindness, Tobias could no longer work and he became very poor. But he kept his soul free from sin and trusted in God.

Then he remembered that he had loaned some money to a friend named Gabelus. This man lived in the town of Rages, which was very far from where Tobias lived.

Now, Tobias had a son, who was also called Tobias. He called for his son and said, "Find some faithful man to go with you to Rages. Go there and collect from Gabelus, my friend, the money which I loaned to him when you were still a child."

Young Tobias did as his father commanded, and he went out to look for some faithful man to go with him to Rages. As he was walking along, he met a handsome young man. Tobias explained to him where he wanted to go, and asked him if he knew the road to Rages.

The young man answered, "I do, and I also know your father's friend, Gabelus, who lives there."

Tobias then took the young man to his father, and the blind Tobias said to him, "Can you take my son to Gabelus at Rages? When you return I will pay you for your trouble."

The young man said that he would take Tobias there and bring him back safely.

When everything was ready, Tobias bade his father and mother farewell, and he and the young man set out on the long journey.

One day while Tobias and his guide were on the journey, Tobias sat down by a river to wash his feet. When he put his feet into the water, a big fish came up. It was so large that it frightened Tobias, and he cried out to the young man for help. His guide said, "Do not be afraid; take the fish by the gills and pull it out of the water."

Tobias pulled the fish out, and then his guide told him to cut out its heart, gall, and liver, and to save them for medicine.

On the way to Rages, Tobias and his guide stopped at the house of a man named Raguel. Raguel had a daughter whose name was Sara. Tobias and Sara grew to love each other very much, and with her father's consent Tobias married her. Raguel gave Tobias one half of his property as a wedding present and made a great wedding feast. While the feast was going on, the guide went to Gabelus and collected the money.

When the wedding feast was over, Tobias and his guide made ready to start for home. Sara's parents bade her good-bye and she went along with Tobias.

After they had been traveling for several days, the guide said to Tobias, "You and I will go ahead. Let the others follow after us. Your father is waiting for you. Take along the gall of the fish, for it will cure blindness."

THE HOMECOMING

At home, the blind Tobias and his wife were waiting for their son. Every day the mother went to the top of the hill to see if he and his guide were coming. At last, one day she saw them while they were still far off. She went home at once to tell her husband that Tobias was coming, and they both went out to welcome him. When they met him, they wept for joy.

The first thing Tobias did was to spread the gall of the fish over his father's eyes. He had no sooner done this than his father's eyes were opened and he could see perfectly.

The young Tobias did not forget his guide. He wanted to pay the young man for his services and offered to give him half of all he owned. But the guide smiled at him and said, "You do not know who I am. I am Raphael, one of the seven angels who stand before God."

When Tobias and his father heard this, they fell down before him. But the angel said to them, "Peace be to you. Fear not. It was God Who sent me to you. Bless Him and praise Him." When he said this, he disappeared and they never saw him again.

Seven days later, Sara arrived with all her servants and the cattle and camels which her father had given Tobias. He and his parents were very glad to see her and they welcomed her with a great feast.

Tobias' father lived to be very old. After he had died, his son stayed with his mother until her death. He buried her near his father, and then he and Sara and their children went to live with Sara's parents.

SUGGESTIONS FOR STUDY

1. FILL IN THE BLANKS WITH THESE WORDS.

gall   Commandments   collect   services   Dirt

a. Tobias loved God and kept the —————.
b. ————— fell into Tobias' eyes and made him blind.
c. When Tobias spread the ————— over his father's eyes he was cured.
d. Young Tobias wanted to pay the guide for his —————.
e. Tobias went to ————— money loaned to his father's friend.

2. CORRECT EACH SENTENCE BY CHANGING *one* WORD.

a. The Assyrians were taken to Assyria.
b. The young Tobias caught a big serpent.
c. The guide said he was Gabriel, an angel.
d. Tobias received half of Sara's property when he married.
e. Tobias' parents thanked Sara that their son was safe.

3. HOW WELL CAN YOU THINK?

a. Young Tobias was always obedient and he loved his parents, caring for them until their death. How does God expect you to act toward your parents? Mention some things you can do to show them that you love them.
b. Some people love God only when they have no trouble. How did Tobias act when he had trouble? How can we imitate him?

4. DO YOU KNOW WHAT THESE WORDS MEAN?

gall	guide	consent
hearth	gills	explained
succeeded	injury	disappear

XIII † DANIEL AND HIS FRIENDS

DANIEL AND THE
KING'S DREAM A king named Nabuchodonosor came to Jerusalem with a very strong
army and conquered it. He captured many Jews and
took them to his kingdom, Babylon, where they were
treated as slaves. There they had to build walls and dig
canals and help build great gardens where the people
of Babylon went to enjoy themselves.

Some of these Israelites were very well educated
and were treated more kindly than the others. Among
these well-educated Israelites was a man named Daniel. He belonged to the tribe of Juda and was from
the family of the king of Israel. He had three friends
who were as learned as he was. Nabuchodonosor liked
Daniel and his three friends and he allowed them to
live as members of his own family.

One night the king had a dream and in the morning
he called all his wise men together and asked them to

explain the dream to him. None of them could explain it, so he ordered all of them to be put to death.

Daniel and his three friends were not present when the king asked the wise men to explain his dream, but the king's soldiers were going to kill them, too. However, Daniel asked to be given some time, for he knew that God would help him to explain the dream.

Daniel and his three friends prayed to God to help them. After that, Daniel went before the king and asked to be allowed to explain the dream. The king gave him permission, and Daniel not only told the king what he dreamed, but also what the dream meant. This astonished the king, and he said that Daniel's God was the true God. Because of these things, Nabuchodonosor made Daniel governor and gave his three friends high positions in Babylon.

DANIEL'S FRIENDS

Some time after this, Nabuchodonosor set up a golden idol. He called all the chief men of Babylon together and told them that they were to worship it. Anyone who did not worship it was to be thrown into a blazing furnace.

Daniel's three young friends refused to honor the idol. This made the king very angry and he ordered

Daniel's friends to be thrown into a furnace heated seven times hotter than usual.

The three young men were bound hand and foot, and the king's servants threw them into the furnace. The men who threw them in were burned to death, but the three young men were not hurt at all. When they were in the furnace, God sent a moist, cool wind and the three young men walked about in the furnace praising God.

After a while the king looked into the fiery furnace. He saw not three, but four young men walking about in it unhurt. The fourth was an angel of the Lord.

This shocked Nabuchodonosor and he knew that God was protecting the three young men. He said, "Blessed is the God of these young men, Who sent His angel to save them. There is no other god that can save like this."

The king then called the young men to come out of the furnace and he again promoted them in his service.

DANIEL IN THE LIONS' PIT

Some years later another king, Darius, ruled Babylon. Darius also liked Daniel and was going to give him a very high place in the kingdom. Some of the other powerful men in the kingdom became very jealous of Daniel when they heard this. They decided to make trouble for him.

These men knew that Daniel prayed to God three times a day. Being very sly, they tricked the king into making a law forbidding everyone in the kingdom to ask God or man for anything during a period of thirty days. Anyone who broke this law was to be cast into a pit full of hungry lions.

Daniel knew all about this law, but he refused to obey it. He prayed every day as usual. Daniel's enemies watched him carefully, and one day they saw him praying. They went to the king and told him that Daniel had broken the law. They demanded that Daniel be thrown into the lions' pit.

The king pitied Daniel and tried to save him. But Daniel's enemies insisted that the king punish him. The king had Daniel taken to the lions' pit. Before he was cast into the pit, the king said: "You have always served God, and He will take care of you."

Then they threw Daniel into the pit and closed it up. The king went back to his palace and was very sad. He felt very bad about what happened to Daniel.

The next morning the king hurried to the lions' pit. "Daniel," he called out, "has God saved you?"

And Daniel answered the king, "O king, my God has kept the lions from hurting me because I did no wrong in disobeying your law."

The king was happy to find out that Daniel was safe. At once, he had Daniel taken out of the pit and he told all the kingdom about how good and powerful God is.

Daniel and his friends were faithful to God's law, and God watched over them.

SUGGESTIONS FOR STUDY

1. WHO AM I?

    a. I was a king of Babylon who conquered Jerusalem.
    b. I explained the king's dream.
    c. I walked about in the furnace with the three young men.
    d. I was the king of Babylon who put Daniel into the pit.
    e. I saved Daniel from the lions.

2. FILL IN THE BLANKS WITH THESE WORDS.

lions   worship   slaves   kindly   wrong

    a. The Israelites were treated like _____ in Babylon.
    b. Daniel and his friends were treated more _____ than the other Israelites.
    c. Daniel's friends would not _____ the golden idol.
    d. The _____ did not harm Daniel at all.
    e. Daniel was saved from the lions because he did no _____.

3. DRAW A LINE UNDER THE CORRECT ANSWER.

    a. (An angel—Daniel) told King Nabuchodonosor what his dream meant.

b. Daniel was put in the lions' pit because the king listened to Daniel's (friends—enemies).
c. (God—The king) saved Daniel from the lions.
d. Nabuchodonosor made Daniel a (governor—teacher).
e. The young men (were—were not) hurt by the fire of the furnace.

4. HOW WELL CAN YOU THINK?

a. God protected Daniel and his friends from their wicked enemies because they trusted in Him. How can you put your trust in God during the day?
b. What wrong thing did Darius do because he gave in to Daniel's enemies? Why should we never be afraid to do right?

5. CAN YOU USE THESE WORDS IN SENTENCES?

position	blazing	sly
empire	furnace	insisted
promoted	forbid	

XIV † QUEEN ESTHER SAVES HER PEOPLE

The Israelites used to tell the story of a beautiful girl named Esther. Her mother and father died when she was a child, so her uncle adopted her. Her uncle's name was Mardochai.

When she was a young girl, Assuerus, or Xerxes, was then the Persian king and he ordered that all the beautiful girls in his kingdom be brought to his palace, for he wanted to select a queen. Esther was one of the girls who was brought there.

For one year the girls lived in the palace before they were brought to the king. They all tried to make themselves more beautiful by dressing in fine garments, using perfumes and wearing beautiful jewels. But Esther did not have to do this, for even in simple clothes she was the most beautiful of the girls.

After a year the king sent for the girls. They went before him one by one. As soon as the king saw Esther, he knew she was the most beautiful girl in the palace. He put a crown on her head and made her queen of the land. Then he made a great feast in her honor and invited many people.

Next to the king, the greatest man in the palace was a prince called Aman. Whenever Aman came into a room everyone had to bow down before him.

Now, Mardochai always remained near the king's palace, for he wanted to be near Esther. But, when he came to the palace, he would not bow down before Aman. This made Aman very angry and he decided he would have all the Jews killed because Mardochai would not bow before him.

Aman went to Assuerus, the king, and told him that the Jews were planning to kill him. Aman said that because of this all the Jews in the kingdom should be killed. The king trusted Aman and placed his ring on Aman's finger and told him to do with the Jews whatever he thought should be done. Then Aman sent messengers to all parts of the kingdom with letters saying that on a certain day all the Jews were to be killed. In all the towns and cities where this letter was read, there was great fright among the Jews.

Mardochai put on sackcloth and went to the gates of the palace. The servants told Esther that her uncle was there dressed in sackcloth. She sent him other

clothes, but he would not wear them. Instead, he sent to her the letter of the king which said that all the Jews should be killed. He asked her to go to the king and beg him to spare her people.

THE KING SPARES ESTHER'S PEOPLE

Not even the queen could go before the king unless she had been sent for. The penalty for violating this law was death. But Esther loved her people and she was ready to die for them if necessary. She sent this message to Mardochai, "Gather all the Jews together in the city and pray for me. Let them fast three days and three nights, and I will do the same. Then I will go before the king. I know that I may be killed for doing this, but I will do it for my people."

On the third day, after Esther had put on her most beautiful dress, she went before the king. The king was seated on his throne and, when he saw Esther standing before him, he was surprised. But the king was not angry with her, because she was so beautiful.

The king held out to her his golden scepter and she kissed the top of it. The king then said to her, "What do you wish? If you should ask me for half of my kingdom, I would give it to you."

The queen answered, "If I have pleased you, my king, come to the feast which I have made for you and Aman."

King Assuerus and Aman went to the feast. At the feast the king again asked, "What is it that you wish, my queen? Even if you ask for half of my kingdom, I will give it to you."

Queen Esther answered, "If I have pleased you, my king, come to the feast which I will make ready for you tomorrow."

Aman was very happy that day because he had feasted with the king and queen. But when he went out of the palace he saw Mardochai sitting at the gate. Mardochai did not bow down before him. This filled

Aman with rage, and he ordered a gallows to be built. He was going to hang Mardochai.

That night the king could not sleep. He sent for his servants and told them to read to him. The servants read to him the story of his kingdom, which told how Mardochai had once saved the king's life when some wicked servants had plotted to kill him. When the king heard this, he asked, "What reward did Mardochai receive?"

The servants answered, "No reward at all."

Just then Aman came and asked to speak to the king. He was going to ask the king to allow him to have Mardochai hanged. When he came in, the king questioned him, "What ought to be done to a man whom the king wishes to honor?"

Aman thought that the king wished to honor him, so he said, "The man whom the king wishes to honor ought to be dressed in the king's garments. He ought to be put upon the king's horse, and have a crown upon his head. The first of the king's princes ought to lead his horse through the streets of the city and cry out to all looking on: 'Honor him, for the king has honored him.'"

The king then replied to Aman, "Make haste, and do all of this to Mardochai the Jew. He is sitting before the gate of the palace."

Aman made haste and did as the king commanded. He led Mardochai riding on the king's horse through the streets of the city. Mardochai wore the king's garments and had a crown on his head and, as they went along, Aman cried out, "Honor him, for the king has honored him."

When it was all over, Aman went home. He was very angry. He told his wife and his friends everything that had happened. While he was talking, a messenger came from the king bidding him to come to the queen's feast.

Aman went and again sat at the table with the king and queen. The king again said to Esther, "What is

your wish, Queen Esther, that I may give it to you? Even if you ask for half of my kingdom, it shall be given to you."

This time Esther was ready to tell the king her wish. She said, "If I have pleased you, my king, give me my life. I ask for my life and the life of my people, for we have an enemy who wants to kill us."

Then the king asked, "Who is your enemy?"

Esther answered, "Aman is our enemy."

Aman was very much ashamed. He hung his head and said nothing.

The king was angry when he heard this. He got up from the table and went into the garden. When the king came back from the garden he commanded the servants to take Aman and hang him. Aman was hanged that day on the gallows which he had built for Mardochai.

The king gave great honors to Mardochai, and the Jews were very happy. They thanked and praised God because He had saved them from the wicked Aman.

SUGGESTIONS FOR STUDY

1. FILL IN THE BLANKS WITH THESE WORDS.

    Jews   Aman   hanged   bow   killed

    a. Esther wanted to save the lives of the _____.
    b. Mardochai would not _____ down before Aman.
    c. The king and _____ were invited to a banquet.
    d. Aman decided to have all the Jews _____.
    e. Aman was _____ on his own gallows.

2. CORRECT EACH SENTENCE BY CHANGING *one* WORD.

    a. Mardochai begged the king to save her life.
    b. The king wished to honor Aman.
    c. Esther put on sackcloth and sat at the gate.
    d. The gallows were built by Mardochai.
    e. Assuerus attended the feast with the king.

3. MATCH COLUMN I WITH COLUMN II.

    a. Mardochai   ( ) built a gallows.
    b. Xerxes   ( ) saved the king's life.
    c. Esther   ( ) was a beautiful girl.
    d. Aman   ( ) was a Persian king.
    e. Assuerus   ( ) is another name for Assuerus.

4. ANSWER YES OR NO.

    a. Mardochai had once saved the king's life.
    b. The king rewarded Mardochai.
    c. The king asked Aman what he should do to honor a certain man.
    d. Aman knew that the man the king remembered was Mardochai.
    e. Aman was pleased to lead Mardochai through the streets of the city.

5. HOW WELL CAN YOU THINK?

   a. Esther pleaded for her people with the king. How does Esther make us think of the Blessed Virgin Mary? Why does Jesus listen to Mary when she asks favors for us?

   b. Esther was a beautiful girl. But more important, her soul was beautiful and pleasing to God. How can you make your soul more beautiful?

6. DO YOU KNOW WHAT THESE WORDS MEAN?

sackcloth	penalty	garments
violating	fright	scepter
clothes	rage	feast

THE COMING

Many, many years had passed since Adam and Eve had disobeyed God and had been driven out of the Garden of Paradise. But the people had not forgotten God had promised them that one day a Savior would come into the world. They remembered what God had told Abraham, that in him all nations would be blessed, and what Jacob had foretold about the Savior of the World springing from the tribe of Juda.

OF OUR SAVIOR

Most of the nations in the world had turned away from God and were worshiping false gods. But God watched over the Israelites and sent them prophets so that they would not forget Him. The Israelites remained true to God and longed for the day when the Savior would come. At last their patience was rewarded. God sent His Only-Begotten Son into the world. "The Word was made flesh and dwelt among us."

THE NEW
TESTAMENT

XV † THE BIRTH
AND CHILDHOOD
OF OUR LORD

ZACHARY IN THE TEMPLE In a little town near the city of Jerusalem there lived a priest named Zachary and his wife Elizabeth. Like all good Jews, they longed for the coming of the Savior and hoped that He would be born of their family. But they were old and they had no son. Living all by themselves, they were lonely. They prayed every day that God would send them a son, so that they would be comforted.

One day it was Zachary's turn, as a priest of the Temple, to offer incense to God. The Altar of Incense was in the Temple. The people knelt outside in the courts of the Temple, while Zachary went inside. The incense was in a golden cup. Zachary took the cup in his hand and poured out the incense on the fire which was burning on the altar. Then he stepped back and watched the great cloud of smoke rise up into the air.

Suddenly, as the smoke cleared, Zachary saw an angel standing at the right side of the altar. He was terribly frightened, but the angel said, "Fear not, Zachary, for the Lord has heard your prayer. You and Elizabeth shall have a son. You shall call him John. He will make you very happy because he will be great before the Lord. He shall prepare the people for the coming of the Savior."

Zachary doubted the angel. He did not see how his words could come true. Then the angel said to him, "I am Gabriel, who stands before God. The Lord sent me to bring you these good tidings. But because you have not believed my word, you shall not be able to speak until the day when these things shall come to pass."

Outside in the court of the Temple the people were praying. They wondered why Zachary stayed so long inside the Temple. At last he came out to them. He tried to speak to them, but could not. He made signs to them to let them know that he had seen a vision, but he remained dumb from that day on.

THE ANGEL GABRIEL VISITS MARY

Now Elizabeth, Zachary's wife, had a cousin named Mary. Mary was very holy. She always obeyed God's commandments and never committed the slightest sin. Her soul was pure.

Mary was engaged to a man named Joseph. He was very poor, and had to work hard at the carpenter's trade to make a living. God had chosen him to watch over Mary and protect her.

Six months after the angel Gabriel had appeared to Zachary in the Temple, God sent him to Nazareth, to the home of Mary. Mary was kneeling in prayer when, all at once, she saw the angel Gabriel standing before her and heard him say, "Hail, full of grace, the Lord is with thee; blessed art thou among women!"

Mary was afraid. She wondered why God should

send an angel to her. She did not know what the
words of the angel meant, but the angel said to her,
"Fear not, Mary, for you have found favor with God.
You shall have a Son and you shall call Him Jesus.
He shall be great and shall be called the Son of the
Most High. The Holy Ghost shall come upon you,
and your Child shall be called the Son of God. Behold,
your cousin Elizabeth shall also have a son."

Mary believed the words of the angel. She knew
that God had sent him. She was willing to do whatever God asked of her, so she said, "Behold the
handmaid of the Lord; be it done to me according to
thy word."

When Mary gave this answer to the angel Gabriel, God became man.

MARY VISITS ELIZABETH

The news that Elizabeth was going to have a son made Mary very happy. She knew that Elizabeth was getting old and was all alone. She made up her mind to go to her and see if she could help her. It was a long, tiresome journey. It led over a high hill and two low valleys, but Mary did not mind the trouble. She was thinking only of Elizabeth.

At last, tired out from her travels, Mary came to the home of Zachary and Elizabeth. Elizabeth was very surprised when she saw her, and a great feeling of happiness came over her. Deep in her heart she heard the voice of the Holy Ghost telling her the wonderful thing that had happened to Mary. She threw her arms around her cousin and said, "Blessed art thou among women, and blessed is the fruit of thy womb. Who am I that the Mother of my Lord should come to me?"

When Mary heard these words of her cousin, she praised God. "My soul praises God," she said, "for all the wonderful things He has done for me. I am lowly and poor but He has lifted me up and made me great. Behold, from this time forward all people shall call me blessed."

Mary stayed with Elizabeth for three months. She waited on her and helped her with the housework. She was very kind to poor Zachary, who could not speak to her, for he was still dumb.

THE BIRTH OF JOHN THE BAPTIST

At last the day came when a son was born to Zachary and Elizabeth as the angel had promised. All their relatives and friends came to see the little baby. They were wondering what name his parents would give him. They thought he should be called Zachary, after his father. But when they asked Zachary what the baby's name should be, he took a writing-tablet and wrote on it, "John is his name." He had no sooner written these words than the power to speak came back to him. He began to praise God for His mercy and His goodness.

THE BIRTH OF OUR LORD

In those days the whole world was governed by the Emperor of Rome. His name was Augustus. He wondered how many subjects he ruled and he made up his mind to find out. He sent out an order for a census to be taken. Everyone was to report his name and the value of his property to the officials.

The Jews at this time were subjects of the Roman Emperor. So, every Jew had to report to the town from which his family came in order to have his name written down. The Blessed Virgin and St. Joseph were living in Nazareth. They went to Bethlehem because it was the city of David, and Joseph and Mary came from the House of David.

In those times traveling was very hard. The roads were bad, but Mary and Joseph knew it was God's will that they should make the journey and they went on their way in peace and joy.

Bethlehem was only a little town and, when Mary and Joseph reached there, they found it crowded. Many people had come to be enrolled there.

Mary and Joseph had no friends to welcome them. They could not even find a place to sleep at night for there was no room in the inn. The only place they could find was a cave outside the city. It was a kind of stable where the animals stayed when the weather was bad.

There Joseph and Mary decided to stay for the night. Mary was very tired from the long journey, and Joseph knew that her time was near.

At midnight in that lonely stable Jesus was born. Mary wrapped Him in swaddling-clothes and laid Him on the straw in a manger. Then Mary and Joseph knelt down and adored the Infant God.

THE SHEPHERDS

When Jesus was born, the people of Bethlehem were sound asleep. In the crowded inn the travelers rested from their journey. Nobody in the town knew about the wonderful thing that had happened in the cave. Out in the country on the hillside a few shepherds were awake. They were keeping the night watch over

their sheep. Suddenly everything became as light as day and the shepherds saw an angel. They were very frightened and wondered what it all meant.

The angel said to them, "Fear not, for I bring you tidings of great joy that shall be to all the people. Today in the town of Bethlehem the Savior of the world is born. This shall be a sign to you. You shall find the Infant wrapped in swaddling-clothes and laid in a manger."

Suddenly a whole army of angels appeared. The shepherds heard them sing, "Glory to God in the highest and on earth peace to men of good will." The sound of their voices filled the air.

When the angels disappeared, the light died out. Everything was dark and quiet once more. The shepherds got over their fright, and they said to one another, "Let us go to Bethlehem and see that which the Lord has made known to us."

The shepherds hastened to Bethlehem. They found the cave and went in as softly and quietly as they could. There they saw Mary and Joseph, and the Infant lying in the manger. The shepherds fell upon their knees and adored God Who had become a little baby.

When morning came, the shepherds left the cave, praising and thanking God. After eight days the Child was circumcised and received the name of Jesus.

JESUS IS PRESENTED IN THE TEMPLE

According to the law of Moses, every Jewish mother had to bring her first-born son to the Temple and offer him to God. When Jesus was forty days old, Mary and Joseph took Him to Jerusalem and brought Him to the Temple. There Mary offered Him to God as the law commanded. The law said that if the child's parents were rich, they had to offer a lamb for the sacrifices in the Temple and a young pigeon or a turtledove. If they could not afford to pay for a lamb, they were to offer two turtledoves or two pigeons. Mary and Joseph were poor, so they offered the turtledoves.

While Mary and Joseph were in the Temple, they met a holy man named Simeon. He had come to the Temple that day because the Holy Spirit had told him that he would see the Savior of the world. Simeon took Jesus in his arms and thanked God for letting him see the Redeemer before he died. He pressed the Infant Savior to his heart and told Mary that many people would hate her Son and would not accept His teachings. He told Mary that she too would have to suffer much. "Your own heart a sword shall pierce," he said to her.

There was also in the Temple a widow named Anna. She was very old and spent her time praying and fasting and waiting for the Savior. When she saw the Infant Jesus, she was very happy and she praised God for His goodness to her. She told everyone that she had seen the Messias in the Temple.

THE WISE MEN BRING GIFTS

Far away in the East there were wise men who studied the stars and tried to learn from them the will of God. The night that Jesus was born in Bethlehem, they saw a wonderful new star in the heavens. They understood that a star would be a sign that the King of the Jews was born. When they saw the star they knew that this great event must have happened.

These wise men, together with their servants and their camels, started out to find this newborn King. They took with them many wonderful gifts. They traveled over mountains and through valleys, across great deserts until they came to Jerusalem. When they entered the city of Jerusalem, the star disappeared. They stopped the people on the street and asked them, "Where is He Who is born King of the Jews? We have seen His star in the East and have come to adore Him."

No one in Jerusalem had heard about a newborn King of the Jews. The people were very much excited. At last the king of Jerusalem, whose name was Herod, found out that the wise men had come and that they were looking for a new King.

Herod called together all the priests and the learned men of the Jews. He asked them if God had ever made known the place where the Messias should be born. The priests studied everything in the sacred books that told about the Savior of the world. They told Herod that the new King would be born in the little town of Bethlehem.

Herod sent for the wise men. He spoke to them and asked them all about the star that they had seen in the East. Then he told them to go to Bethlehem. "When you find the Child," he said, "come back and tell me, for I, too, wish to adore Him."

The wise men thanked the king and went on their way. As soon as they had left Jerusalem, the star again appeared. They were very happy when they saw it. It went before them and finally stopped over the house where the Child Jesus was. The wise men went into the house and there they found the Infant Jesus with His Mother. Falling down, they adored Him. They offered Him gold, frankincense and myrrh.

The wise men stayed in Bethlehem that night. They made up their minds to go back to Jerusalem the next morning to tell Herod where he could find the newborn King. While they slept, God told them not to return to Herod, but to go back to their homes by another road.

Herod waited and waited for the wise men to come back to Jerusalem. One day after another passed and they did not come. Then Herod knew that they had gone home. He was very angry.

Herod was jealous. He was afraid that this new King of the Jews would take his place. He was a cruel man and did not think any deed too wicked that would help him to get what he wanted. At first he did not know what to do. Then, he began to think about what the wise men said.

From what the wise men had told him, he knew that the Child could not be any more than two years old. So he sent his soldiers into Bethlehem and ordered them to kill every little boy who was two years old or younger. The soldiers came to Bethlehem and snatched all the baby boys from their mothers' arms and killed them. There was great weeping and mourning in the little town of Bethlehem. The Church calls these children who were killed in this cruel way the Holy Innocents.

Herod's soldiers did not find Jesus. An angel of the Lord had spoken to Joseph while he was sleeping and said to him, "Rise, take the Child and His Mother and go into Egypt. Stay there until I shall tell you to return, for Herod is going to seek the Child and try to kill Him."

In the middle of the night, Joseph arose, took Jesus and His Mother and set out on the long, hard journey to Egypt. It was while they were living there that Jesus began to walk and talk.

Then, one night an angel spoke to Joseph once more. He said, "Take the Child and His Mother and return to the land of Israel. They who sought to kill Him are dead." So the Holy Family went back to Israel. They did not go to Bethlehem, for Herod's son was now the king and he, too, was a cruel man. They settled down to live in another section, Galilee, in the town of Nazareth. Here Mary and Joseph had lived before Jesus was born. Here the angel had appeared to Mary and had told her that she was to be the Mother of God.

In Nazareth Jesus grew up like any other Jewish boy. The people in the town did not know that God was living there. Jesus was obedient to Mary and

Joseph. He was getting ready for the great work that His Father wanted Him to do here on earth.

JESUS IN THE TEMPLE

Today there are many churches in which the Holy Sacrifice of the Mass is offered to God. You can find a church in the smallest town, and in some large cities there are more than a hundred churches.

But when Jesus was a little boy there was only one great church in the whole world where sacrifice was offered to God. This was the Temple in Jerusalem. In other towns there were buildings where the people came together to pray and to listen to sermons and instructions. These were called synagogues. On the Sabbath Day the people went to the synagogue to learn about God and about the Savior Who was to come into the world. But they did not offer sacrifices in the synagogue. There they prayed and heard the law of Moses explained by the leader, or chief of the synagogue.

On great feast days, they traveled to Jerusalem and went up to the Temple to be present at the sacrifices. Thousands of Jews went up to the Temple every year to celebrate the feast of the Pasch. This feast reminded them of the time when God spared the first-born of the

Israelites, and when Moses led the Children of Israel out of Egypt.

Jesus was twelve years old when Mary and Joseph took Him with them to Jerusalem to celebrate the feast of the Pasch. The feast lasted for seven days. Thousands of animals were sacrificed on the altar to show that the people adored God and thanked Him and that they were sorry for their sins. The people asked God to bless them and to help them in all their needs. They praised God by singing hymns.

When the feast was over, the Jews went back to their own towns. The men and the women did not travel together. The men went in one party, the women in another.

When Mary and Joseph were ready to go home, they joined their friends and relatives who lived in Nazareth, but Jesus remained in Jerusalem. Mary thought that He was with Joseph. Joseph did not miss Him because he thought He was with Mary.

After they had traveled a whole day, Joseph left the men and went to see if he could do anything for Mary. You can imagine how surprised they both were when they found out that Jesus was not with them. They looked for Him everywhere. They asked all their friends and relatives if they had seen Him. But no one knew where He was. So Mary and Joseph

started back to Jerusalem. Their hearts were full of
sorrow because they had lost their Son. For two days
they looked for Him along the way and in the city
of Jerusalem. They searched and searched but could
not find Him.

Two days passed and they had almost given up
hope of finding Jesus again. On the third day they
went up to the Temple to seek Him. There they saw
Jesus. He was sitting among the men whose work it
was to study the law of God and to teach it to the
people. He was listening to these great teachers. He
asked them many questions. They too asked Him
questions and they could not understand how a

twelve-year-old boy could know as much as Jesus knew.

When Joseph and Mary saw Jesus there in the midst of these learned men, they wondered. Mary went up to Him and said, "Son, why have You done this to us? Your father and I have sought You sorrowing."

Jesus said to them, "Why is it that you sought Me? Did you not know that I must be about My Father's business?"

Mary kept these words in her heart. She thought of them very often. She knew that Jesus was the Son of God and that He stayed in the Temple because He was doing His Father's will.

Jesus left Jerusalem with Mary and Joseph and went home to Nazareth. He loved Mary and Joseph and tried to help them in every way He could. He was obedient to them. He advanced in wisdom and age and grace with God and men. He learned the carpenter's trade from Joseph, and after Joseph died He took care of Mary, His Mother.

SUGGESTIONS FOR STUDY

1. WHO SAID THIS AND TO WHOM?

   a. "Hail, full of grace, the Lord is with thee."
   b. "John is his name."
   c. "Behold the handmaid of the Lord."
   d. "Glory to God in the highest."
   e. "Blessed art thou among women."

2. MATCH COLUMN I WITH COLUMN II.

   a. Holy Innocents   (   ) spoke to Joseph in his sleep.
   b. An angel   (   ) came to adore Jesus in Bethlehem.
   c. John   (   ) told Mary she would suffer much.
   d. Shepherds   (   ) were killed by Herod's soldiers.
   e. Simeon   (   ) was given his name by an angel.

3. ANSWER YES OR NO.

   a. Did the wise men return to Herod?
   b. Did Anna know that the Infant Jesus was the Messias?
   c. Did Zachary believe the angel right away?
   d. Was Mary willing to do what God asked her?
   e. Was Elizabeth Mary's sister?

4. FILL IN THE BLANKS WITH THESE WORDS.

   obedient   Gabriel   prepared   Joseph   shepherds

   a. Jesus learned the carpenter's trade when He was a boy from
   —————.
   b. ————— was sent to Mary and to Zachary.
   c. John ————— the people for the coming of the Messias.
   d. Jesus was ————— to Mary and Joseph.
   e. The angels told the ————— of the birth of Jesus in the town of Bethlehem.

5. DRAW A LINE UNDER THE CORRECT ANSWER.

   a. God had chosen (Gabriel—Joseph) to watch over and protect Mary.
   b. Mary went to help (Elizabeth—Anna).
   c. (An angel—The Holy Ghost) told Elizabeth about the wonderful thing that had happened to Mary.
   d. (Herod—Simeon) was afraid that the new King of the Jews would take his place.
   e. Joseph and Mary found Jesus in the (Temple—synagogue).

6. HOW WELL CAN YOU THINK?

   a. Jesus said to Mary, "Did you not know that I must be about My Father's business?" Who is Jesus' Father? What did Jesus mean by "My Father's business?"
   b. Jesus was always obedient to Joseph and Mary even though He was God. What can we learn from this?
   c. The Jews sacrificed animals to show that they adored God, thanked Him for His goodness, and were sorry for their sins. They also asked God for His blessings. What sacrifice is offered today and every day that thanks God for His goodness?
   d. Mary did not tell anyone about the great thing that had happened to her. Instead, she hurried off to help her cousin, Elizabeth. How can we imitate Mary in this respect?

7. CAN YOU USE THESE WORDS IN SENTENCES?

incense	census	emperor
tablet	manger	Messias
synagogue	swaddling	pierce
imitate	sermon	instruction

XVI † OUR LORD BEGINS HIS PUBLIC LIFE

When Jesus was thirty years old, He said farewell to His home in Nazareth and set out to do the work for which He had come into the world. His heavenly Father had sent Him to preach to the people and to win their hearts to God. He came to show us how to live. He came to die for us and to save us from our sins.

But before He began His work, Jesus went to the river Jordan to see His cousin, John the Baptist. John had left his home and Zachary and Elizabeth, his parents, when he was a boy. He went out to live alone in the desert. The only clothing he had was a rough garment made from the skin of a camel. He spent much time praying and doing penance. He ate nothing but wild locusts and honey. God had called him to get the people ready to listen to the preaching of Jesus. When John was thirty years old he came out of the desert and went to the banks of the river Jordan. He chose a place that the people had to pass on their way to Jerusalem. Whenever travelers came by, he stopped them and told them to do penance for their sins. He told them that the Savior had come into the world.

It was not long before everyone in Jerusalem and in the country roundabout had heard of this new prophet who preached on the banks of the river Jordan. Great crowds went out to hear him. When he spoke to them, they felt ashamed of their sins and asked God to forgive them. They wanted to do penance.

After John would finish preaching to them, he would go out into the shallow water of the river. The people stood in line and one by one they went out to where John was standing and he baptized them. God was making their hearts ready for the coming of His Son Who would take away all their sins.

When Jesus came to the Jordan, He stood in the crowd and listened to the words of His cousin. When the time came for the people to be baptized by John, Jesus took His place in line with the rest of the crowd.

At last it was Jesus' turn to be baptized. John looked at Him and knew at once that He was the Savior of the world. He said to Jesus, "I should be baptized by You, and yet, You come to me?"

Jesus answered, "Let it be so, for it is right for us to do everything that My Father wants us to do."

John obeyed and baptized Jesus. Suddenly he saw the heavens open and the Holy Ghost came down in the form of a dove and rested on Jesus. Then a voice from Heaven said, "This is My beloved Son in Whom I am well pleased."

JESUS IS TEMPTED BY THE DEVIL

After Jesus was baptized, the Holy Spirit led Him out into the desert. He stayed there for forty days and forty nights. Jesus prayed and fasted during this time. He was alone and had only wild beasts for His companions.

After forty days, Jesus was very hungry. Then the devil came to Him and said, "If You are the Son of God, command that these stones be made into bread." Jesus answered, "Not by bread alone does man live, but by every word that comes from the mouth of God."

The devil was not satisfied. He was afraid of Jesus and wanted to lead Him into sin. So he took Him to Jerusalem and set Him on the highest part of the Temple. Far below they could see the crowds walking about. The devil said to Jesus, "If You are the Son of

God, cast Yourself down. It is written that angels will bear You up and keep You from dashing Your foot against a stone." Jesus answered, "You shall not tempt the Lord your God."

Still the devil was not discouraged. He tried a third time. He took Jesus to the top of a very high mountain. He showed Him all the kingdoms of the world and said to Jesus, "All this will I give You if falling down You will adore me."

Jesus said, "Begone, Satan; the Lord, your God, you shall adore and Him alone shall you serve." Then the devil went away and angels came and took care of Jesus.

THE FIRST FOLLOWERS OF JESUS

When Jesus left the desert, He came back to the river Jordan. Large crowds of people were listening to the preaching of John. John saw Jesus coming. He pointed to Him and said to the people, "Behold, the Lamb of God. Behold, He it is Who shall take away the sins of the world." Jesus did not stop. He passed on until He came to a little woods. Here He found a hut that had been built by some of the people who had come to listen to the preaching of John. He went into it and rested that night.

The next day Jesus came back to the river Jordan. John was alone with two young men who had come to learn about the kingdom of God. Their names were Andrew and John. When John the Baptist saw Jesus, he said to them, "Behold the Lamb of God." Andrew and John heard these words, and they left John the Baptist to follow Jesus.

Jesus heard their footsteps behind Him. He turned to them and said, "What are you seeking?" The two young men were surprised by this question. They had no answer ready. They said to Jesus, "Master, where do You live?"

Jesus answered, "Come and see."

They went with Jesus to the little hut in the woods. They stayed with Him all that day. He spoke to them about the Kingdom of God and about His Father in Heaven. They were very happy. In the evening they went to tell their friends about Jesus.

Andrew and John were fishermen, but they had left their nets to listen to the preaching of John the Baptist. Now, Andrew had a brother named Simon. Andrew went to find Simon, and the next day he brought him to Jesus. Jesus looked at him and said, "Your name is Simon but it shall be Peter." Simon did not understand what this meant, nor did he know that he was to be the head of the Church.

Jesus told Simon and Andrew and John that He was going to Galilee, and they made up their minds to go with Him. On their way they met a man named Philip. Jesus looked at Philip and said, "Follow Me." Philip obeyed and became the fourth companion of the Savior.

Then Philip went to find another young man named Nathanael, and he found him sitting under a fig-tree. Philip said to Nathanael, "We have found Him of Whom Moses and the prophets wrote. He is Jesus of Nazareth."

Nathanael said in scorn, "Can anything good come out of Nazareth?" Philip said, "Come and see."

When Jesus saw Nathanael coming to Him, He said to His companions, "Here indeed is a true Israelite." Nathanael was surprised to hear these words of Jesus. He wondered how Jesus had known anything about him. Jesus said to him, "Long before Philip called you, Nathanael, I saw you sitting under the fig-tree."

When Nathanael heard this he threw himself on his knees before Jesus and cried, "Master, You are the Son of God. You are the King of Israel."

Andrew and John, Simon, Philip and Nathanael were the first ones to follow the Savior. They were the first disciples of Jesus.

JESUS CHANGES WATER INTO WINE

Some friends of Jesus were going to be married in a little town called Cana, in Galilee. Jesus had been invited and He knew that Mary, His Mother, would be there. It was for this reason that He went to Cana.

There was a great crowd at the wedding feast. More guests came than the bridegroom had expected. He saw that there would not be enough wine to last to the end of the feast. He was very worried because he did not want his guests to feel that they were not welcome.

Mary, the Mother of Jesus, noticed that the bridegroom was troubled and she knew the cause of it. She felt sorry for him, so she went to Jesus and said to Him softly, "They have no wine."

Jesus answered, "What is that to Me and to you? My hour is not yet come."

But Mary knew the love of Jesus and that His heart was tender toward anyone in trouble. She knew that He would answer her prayer, so she said to the waiters, "Do whatever He shall tell you to do."

There were six large stone water-pots standing near the door. Whenever the Jews came into a house they used to wash their hands and feet. That is why the water-pots were there.

Jesus said to the waiters, "Fill the water-pots with water." They filled them up to the brim. Then Jesus said to them, "Now, take out and carry a measure to the chief steward of the feast." They did as He commanded and carried what they had drawn out to the steward. The steward tasted it. It was the finest wine that had been served. He did not know where it came from, so he called the bridegroom and said to him, "Every man serves the good wine first, but you have saved the good wine until now."

Jesus worked His first miracle. Because His Mother had asked Him, He changed water into wine.

THE MIRACULOUS CATCH OF FISHES

Some time after the wedding feast in Cana, Jesus was walking along the shores of the Sea of Galilee. Great crowds of people followed Him. They gathered all around Him, eager to hear His words. There were two fishing-boats standing by the shore. One of them belonged to Simon Peter. Simon Peter was on the shore, washing his nets beside one of the boats. Jesus stepped into the boat near Peter and said, "Row off a little distance from the shore." Simon Peter obeyed, and Jesus sat in the boat and preached to the crowds of people who were standing on the shore.

After a while Jesus had finished talking to the people. He said to Simon Peter, "Now, row out to the middle of the water and let down your nets for a catch."

Simon Peter and Andrew had been fishing all night long and they had caught nothing. That morning they had come back to the land tired and disappointed. So Simon Peter said to Jesus, "Master, we have labored all night and have taken nothing, but at Your word I will let down the net." He called his brother Andrew and they rowed out to the middle of the water.

Simon Peter and Andrew did not hesitate, because Jesus told them to let down the net. When they pulled it up, they were so many fishes in it that the net broke. They called to John, and James, his brother, who were in another boat, to come and help them. There were so many fishes in the net that they filled both boats until they almost sank. Imagine how surprising it would be to make so great a catch of fish.

Simon Peter knew that Jesus had performed a miracle.

Peter fell down at the feet of Jesus and said, "Depart from me, O Lord, for I am a sinful man." Like Peter, Andrew, James and John were also filled with wonder at the great number of fishes that had been caught.

Jesus said to Simon Peter, "Fear not, for I will make you a fisher of men." So they all left their boats and their nets and followed Jesus.

THE TWELVE APOSTLES

Many young men, after they had heard Jesus preach, gave up everything they owned and left their homes and followed Him. They became disciples of Jesus. He sent them into all the little towns to tell the people that He was coming. He gave them the power to cure the sick.

Jesus chose twelve of these disciples to be His special friends. He gave them more power than He gave to the others. These were the Twelve Apostles. They were: Simon Peter and his brother Andrew; James and his brother John; Philip, and Bartholomew, who was sometimes called Nathanael; Thomas and Matthew; James, the son of Alpheus; Jude, or Thaddeus; Simon and Judas Iscariot. Judas Iscariot took care of the money that the people gave to Jesus and His apostles.

THE SICK ARE HEALED

In Cana, a very important man of the neighborhood came to see Jesus. His son was very sick and he asked Jesus to cure him. Jesus said, "Go your way. Your son lives" and the man went home.

When he got home, the man found out that his son

had become well while he was talking to Jesus miles away. The man rejoiced and believed in Jesus.

Capharnaum is a town on the shores of the Sea of Galilee. There lived at Capharnaum a Roman centurion. This centurion was in command of the Roman soldiers who guarded the town. The Jews liked him because he was a good man.

The centurion had a servant whom he loved very much. The servant fell sick and grew worse and worse. The doctors told the centurion that the servant was dying, that he had no chance to get well. But the centurion had heard of Jesus' power to work miracles.

He made up his mind to go to Jesus and ask Him to cure his servant. Jesus was staying in Capharnaum at the time. The centurion went to Him and said, "Lord, my servant is at home dying."

Jesus said to him, "I will come and heal him."

The centurion thought this was too much to expect of Jesus, so he said, "Lord, I am not worthy that You should enter under my roof, but only say the word and my servant shall be healed."

The faith of the centurion made Jesus glad. He said to the Jews who were standing around, "Not even in Israel, have I found such great faith." Then he said to the centurion, "Go, and as you have believed, so shall it be done," and at that moment the centurion's servant was made well.

Another miracle which Jesus worked in Capharnaum surprised the Jews. Jesus was preaching in a house in the town. All the people flocked to see and hear Him, and the room where He sat became crowded. Even the doorway of the house was so jammed with people that it was almost impossible to get through to Jesus.

One of these who wanted to see Jesus was a sick man, who could not move any part of his body. He was carried on a litter by four men. The men saw that they could not get the sick person through the crowded doorway. They went up to the roof of the house and lowered the litter through a large opening in the roof. Jesus was pleased at the faith of the men and the sick person. Jesus said to the man on the litter, "Son, your sins are forgiven."

Some of the chief Jews of the town were present and they thought to themselves, "Why does he say this? Who can forgive sins but God?"

Jesus knew their thoughts and said to them, "Which is easier to say to this sick man, 'Your sins are forgiven,' or 'Arise, take up your litter and walk'? That you may know that the Son of Man has power on earth to forgive sins," Jesus said, turning to the sick man, "Take up your litter and go home." Immediately, the man got up and left, praising God.

One Sabbath day Jesus was teaching in the synagogue and an old sick woman came up to Him. Jesus put his hands on her and she was made well again. The chief of the synagogue got angry and told the people not to come to Jesus to be healed on the Sabbath.

Jesus answered "Does not each one of you give water to your ass or ox on the Sabbath day? Should not this woman be made well on the Sabbath?" The officials did not know what to say.

One day Jesus came to a little town called Naim. His disciples were with Him and a great crowd of people was following Him. At the gate of the city they met a little procession. People were carrying the lifeless body of a young man out of the city to the tomb where they would bury him. The young man had been his mother's only child and she was a widow.

Jesus came near. He told the men who were carrying the litter upon which the body was placed to put it down on the ground. He went up to the poor, sorrowing mother and said to her, "Weep not." Then He put His hand on the dead man. He said, "Young man, I say to you, arise." Even as He spoke, the young man who had been dead sat up and began to speak. Jesus gave him to his mother.

When the people saw this, they were frightened. Never before had they seen such a wonderful deed. They praised God for the great Prophet who had come among them. They told everyone the story of how Jesus had raised the young man to life, and soon the news had spread to every part of the country, and people flocked to see Jesus.

Jesus raised many people from the dead. The young

man, and a young woman, the daughter of the ruler of a synagogue, were both dead for a short time before he brought them back to life. But others, such as Lazarus, were dead for a long time before Jesus restored them.

Lazarus was the brother of Mary and Martha. They were very good friends of Jesus. The sisters sent Jesus a message asking Him to come and see Lazarus, who was very sick, but by the time Jesus got to Bethany, where they lived, Lazarus was dead and buried in the tomb for four days.

Martha went out to meet Jesus and He said to her, "Your brother shall arise."

Martha said, "Yes Lord, I know he will rise at the resurrection on the last day."

Jesus replied, "I am the resurrection and the life. He who believes in Me, even if he die, shall live. Whoever lives and believes in Me shall never die. Do you believe this?"

Martha said to Him, "Yes Lord, I believe that you are the Christ, the Son of God."

Jesus then went to the tomb of Lazarus and when it was opened, He called, "Lazarus come forth." At once Lazarus came out of the tomb, and the people watching the miracle unwrapped the linens that bound the risen man.

A SINNER IS FORGIVEN

Mary Magdalen was a beautiful young girl. She was very rich, but she was also very wicked. She had lovely clothes and wore the finest jewels. She was a vain and proud woman. Good people did not even want to be seen with her, but she did not care what people thought about her.

Mary Magdalen had heard about Jesus. She made up her mind to go and listen to His preaching. She did not want to give up her sinful ways; she only wanted to see what sort of person He was. But when she heard the words of Jesus, her heart was filled with sorrow for her sins. Jesus saw her in the crowd and looked at her. It was not an angry look, but a look of forgiveness and love. Mary Magdalen made up her mind to give up her sinful life and go to Jesus and ask Him to forgive her.

One day a rich man asked Jesus to come and have dinner with him. Jesus accepted the invitation. When Mary Magdalen heard that Jesus was having dinner in the house of the rich man, she thought it would be a good time to go to Him and confess her sins. She laid aside her fine clothes and her jewelry and put on an old, coarse dress. She took a box of her finest perfumes and went to the rich man's house.

The dinner was really a great banquet. There were many guests in the large dining hall. Mary Magdalen forced her way into the room. When the guests saw her, they were very angry. Some of them tried to stop her, but she pushed right by them. She was thinking only of Jesus. She looked up and down the table until she saw Him. Then she rushed to Him and threw herself at His feet. Tears were running down her cheeks and they fell upon the feet of Jesus. She washed His feet with her tears and dried them with her hair. Then she kissed His feet and poured the rich perfume over them.

The rich man and his guests were shocked when

they saw Mary Magdalen kneeling at the feet of Jesus. They said to themselves, "If this Man were a prophet He would know that this woman is a sinner." But Jesus read their thoughts. He said to the rich man, "I have something to say to you." The rich man said, "Master, say it."

Jesus then told a story: "A certain man had two men who owed him money. One owed him ten times as much as the other. He felt sorry for them and told them that they would not have to pay their debt. Which of the two loved him more?"

The rich man said, "I suppose the one that owed him the more money."

Jesus said, "You judged rightly." Then He turned to Mary Magdalen. "Do you see this woman?" He asked. "When I entered your house, you gave Me no water to wash My feet. She has washed My feet with her tears. You gave Me no kiss of welcome. She has not stopped kissing My feet. You did not anoint My head. She has anointed My feet. I say to you, many sins are forgiven her because she has loved much." Then Jesus turned to Mary Magdalen and said to her, "Go in peace. Your sins are forgiven."

SUGGESTIONS FOR STUDY

I. UNDERLINE THE CORRECT ANSWER.

   a. John the Baptist was a (priest—prophet—savior).
   b. Jesus cured the man on the litter in (Bethany—Capharnaum —Cana).
   c. Jesus chose (ten—eleven—twelve) apostles.
   d. Jesus called (Philip—Andrew—Nathanael) a true Israelite.

2. WHO SAID THIS AND TO WHOM?

   a. "Yes Lord, I believe that you are the Christ."
   b. "If you are the Son of God, cast yourself down."
   c. "Your name is Simon but it shall be Peter."
   d. "They have no wine."
   e. "Lord I am not worthy that you should enter under my roof."

3. FILL IN THE BLANKS WITH THESE WORDS.

   miracle   servant   Lazarus   Galilee   Jordan

a. John the Baptist preached on the banks of the —————.
b. Jesus healed the centurion's —————.
c. Jesus told ————— to come forth from the tomb.
d. Jesus worked his first ————— at Cana.
e. Peter and Andrew cast their nets into the sea of —————.

4. HOW WELL CAN YOU THINK?

a. Jesus allowed the devil to tempt Him in order to teach us how to act when we are tempted. What does Jesus wish us to do when we are tempted? Is a temptation a sin?
b. Jesus changed water into wine at the wedding feast. What change takes place in the Mass? Can you see this change?
c. Jesus waited in line to be baptized by John the Baptist. He wished to teach us to be humble. How can we best prepare ourselves to receive such sacraments as Penance and the Holy Eucharist?

5. DO YOU KNOW WHAT THESE WORDS MEAN?

shallow	disciple	banquet
restore	centurion	steward
locust	scorn	neighborhood
vain	litter	glimpse

XVII † MORE PARABLES AND MIRACLES

J esus came to save sinners. He never grew tired of telling them that He loved them. He wanted them to be sorry for their sins so that His Father would forgive them and they could be happy with Him in Heaven. He did not want them to lose their souls. One day He told the people a beautiful story which showed just how much he loved them and which pointed out just how much He would do for them and their children.

There was a shepherd who had a hundred sheep. He led them to the finest pasture and watched over them so that nothing would hurt them. Once, when they were crossing a desert, one of the sheep wandered away. The shepherd counted his flock and there were only ninety-nine sheep. So, He left the ninety-nine sheep in the desert and started out to look for the one that had strayed away.

He looked for the lost sheep all day, but could not find it. He looked for it all night, too. Only the next morning did he find his lost sheep. He put his arms around it and held it close to his heart. He laid it on his shoulders and carried it back to the flock. When he reached home, he called all his friends together and said, "I am very happy and I want you to be happy, too, because I have found my sheep that was lost."

For fear that the crowd might not understand just what He meant by this story, Jesus said, "So there shall be more joy in Heaven over one sinner who does penance, than over ninety-nine who do not need to do penance."

THE SERMON ON THE MOUNT

Jesus taught the people by telling them stories, or parables. He also taught them by means of simple sayings which the people could remember.

One day when He saw the crowds that were following Him, He went up on a mountain, and when He was seated and all the people were around Him, sitting or lying on the grass, He taught them saying:

"Blessed are the poor in spirit, for theirs is the Kingdom of Heaven."

"Blessed are the meek, for they shall possess the earth."

"Blessed are they who mourn, for they shall be comforted."

"Blessed are they who hunger and thirst for justice, for they shall be satisfied."

"Blessed are the merciful, for they shall obtain mercy."

"Blessed are the clean of heart, for they shall see God."

"Blessed are the peacemakers, for they shall be called children of God."

"Blessed are they who suffer persecution for justice sake, for theirs is the kingdom of Heaven."

"Blessed are you, when men reproach you, and persecute you, and speaking falsely, say all manner of evil against you for my sake. Rejoice and exult, because your reward is great in Heaven."

When Jesus had finished the people knew that he was teaching them new things.

THE GOOD SAMARITAN

One day when Jesus was telling the people that they must love their neighbor, a certain lawyer asked Him, "Who is my neighbor?"

Jesus then told a story. He told the people about a certain man who was going from Jerusalem to Jericho. On the way he met some thieves who robbed and beat him. They left him half-dead by the roadside.

After a while a priest came by, and seeing the man lying there, he passed on. Soon after a Levite came along the same road, but he also passed by the poor man. Finally, a certain Samaritan came along. When he saw the man, he went over and bound up his wounds and brought him to a nearby inn by putting him on the back of his own donkey. There he took care of him. The next day he gave the innkeeper two silver pieces and said, "Take care of him, and if you spend more than this, I will repay you when I come back this way."

Jesus then asked, "Which of the three proved himself the neighbor of the man who was robbed?"

The man who asked Jesus the question in the first place said, "He who took pity on him." And Jesus said, "Go and do likewise."

THE PRODIGAL SON

Jesus told the people another story. This one explained why God does not hate sinners but wants them to give up their sins and be good.

The story was about a man who had two sons. The older son loved his home and wanted to be near his father. He worked very hard and never caused his father any worry.

The younger son did not like to stay at home. He said to his father, "Give me my share of your property. I am tired of living at home. I want to go out and see the world."

This made his father sad. He knew his son was making a mistake, but he did not want to force him to stay at home against his will. So he gave him his share of the property, and the younger son left home and went far away.

He came to a strange city and made many friends. But they were not true friends. They did not care about the young man; they only wanted his money.

Soon his money was spent, and all his new friends left him. Then a great famine swept over the land. He went to his friends for help, but they would not listen to him. At last when he was almost starving, a man hired him to feed pigs. He was so hungry that he ate the husks that were thrown to the pigs.

Then he began to think of his home. He thought of the servants in his father's house. They had plenty to eat, and he was starving. "I will go back to my father," he said. "I will say, 'Father, I have sinned against Heaven and before you. I am not worthy to be called your son. Let me be one of your servants.'"

So he got up and started on the road for home. When he was yet a great way off, his father saw him. His father had been lonesome for him and had watched every day for him to come home. When he saw him coming, he ran out to meet him. He threw his arms around him and kissed him.

The son said, "Father, I have sinned against Heaven and before you. I am not worthy to be called your son."

But his father told the servants to get out the best clothes in the house. He put shoes on his son's feet and a ring on his finger. He told them to kill the fatted calf and to make a great feast. He was happy because the son that had been lost was found.

Jesus said, "There is joy in Heaven when one sinner does penance."

JESUS QUIETS THE STORM AT SEA

One day Jesus had been preaching and healing the sick all day long. In the evening He was very tired, so He left the crowd and got into a boat with His disciples in order to rest. He said, "Let us go over to the other side of the lake."

They were about halfway across the Sea of Galilee when suddenly a great storm came up. The wind blew harder and harder. Soon there rose great waves which dashed over the boat. The disciples were fishermen and were used to storms, but they had never seen a storm like this one. They feared the boat would sink.

All the while, Jesus was sound asleep in the stern of the boat. The disciples came to Him and woke Him up. They said, "Lord, save us, or we perish."

Jesus said to them. "Why are you afraid, O you of little faith?"

Then He stood up in the boat and raised His hand over the raging water. He said to the storm, "Peace, be still." No sooner had He spoken than the wind stopped blowing, the waves disappeared and a great calm came over the sea.

When the disciples saw this, they were amazed. They said to one another, "Who is this that the winds and the sea obey Him?"

THE LOAVES AND FISHES

The people were always very eager to be with Jesus and to listen to His words. Whenever they heard that He was in some city or out in the country, they all flocked to Him. Once a great crowd followed Him

out into the desert. There Jesus told them all about His Father and Heaven. He healed the sick and comforted those who were in trouble.

Later in the day, His disciples said, "Master, we are here in the desert and there is nothing to eat. Send these people away. Tell them to go into the towns and villages where they can find lodging and buy food to eat."

"They have no need to go," replied Jesus; "you give them to eat."

There were about five thousand men besides the women and children. Turning to Philip, Jesus said: "Where shall we buy bread so all these may eat?" Philip said, "Two hundred silver pieces would not buy enough bread to give everyone just a litttle."

"How many loaves have you?" asked Jesus.

Andrew said, "There is a boy here who has five barley loaves and two fishes, but what are these among so many?"

Jesus said to His disciples, "Tell the people to sit down on the grass."

When they were seated, Jesus stood before them. The people were all waiting to see what He would do. He took the five barley loaves and the two fishes, looked up to Heaven and gave thanks, blessed the bread, broke it and gave it to His disciples. He told them to give it to the people. He did the same with the two fishes.

Five thousand men, besides the women and children, took the loaves and the fishes which the disciples gave them. Every one of them had more than enough to eat.

When they had finished eating, Jesus told the disciples to gather up what was left lest it be lost. The disciples did as Jesus commanded and gathered twelve baskets of what was left of the five loaves and two fishes.

When the people saw the wonderful thing that Jesus had done, they said, "This is indeed the Prophet that has come into the world. Let us take Him and make Him King."

But Jesus knew that they were thinking only of the food He had given them to eat. They thought His Kingdom was of this world. So He fled from them and went up into a mountain to pray.

JESUS WALKS ON THE WATER

Now, when evening had come, the disciples got ready to cross the Sea of Galilee in their boat. Jesus was not with them. They thought He was still praying on the mountain. A violent storm was coming up and after they had gone out on the rough sea, they saw someone walking toward them on the water. They could hardly believe their eyes and they were frightened. They thought it was a ghost, but when they came closer they saw it was Jesus.

Jesus said to them, "Fear not, it is I."

Peter said, "Lord, if it be You, bid me to come to You upon the water."

Jesus said, "Come."

Peter climbed out of the boat and started to walk across the water to Jesus. But the wind was blowing and the waves were high and Peter became afraid. He began to sink down into the water and he cried out, "Lord, save me." Jesus stretched out His hand and took hold of Peter. He said, "O you of little faith, why did you doubt?"

Then they got into the boat and started for the other shore. At once the wind ceased. All of those who were in the boat knelt down and adored Jesus, saying, "Truly, you are the Son of God."

PETER IS MADE HEAD OF THE CHURCH

One day when Jesus and His apostles were walking along, He turned to them and asked, "Who do men say I am?"

They answered, "Some people think You are John the Baptist. Others say You are Elias. Some think You are a great prophet."

Jesus asked, "Who do you think I am?" Peter answered in the name of all the rest. He said, "Thou art Christ, the Son of the living God."

Jesus was very happy when Peter made this act of faith. He said to him, "Blessed are you, Simon, son of John, for flesh and blood has not told you that I am the Son of God, but My Father Who is in Heaven. I say to you that you are Peter, a rock, and upon this rock I will build My Church. The power of Hell shall not harm it. Whatever you shall bind on earth shall be bound in Heaven, and whatever you shall loose on earth shall be loosed in Heaven."

JESUS ON THE MOUNTAIN

At another time Jesus took Peter, James and John with Him to the top of a high mountain. When they got to the top of the mountain, Jesus prayed. All of a sudden, a great change came over Him. His clothes became as white as snow and His face began to shine like the sun. Two men appeared, one to the right of Him and one to the left and they began to speak with Him. These men were Moses and Elias.

When the three apostles saw Jesus so powerful and so glorious, and Moses and Elias with Him, they were very happy. Peter cried out, "Lord, it is good for us to be here. Let us make three little houses, one for You, one for Moses and one for Elias."

While Peter was still speaking, a great cloud covered the whole top of the mountain. From out of the cloud they heard a voice saying, "This is My beloved Son in Whom I am well pleased. Hear ye Him!"

When the apostles heard the voice out of the cloud, they fell on their faces in fear of the Lord. Then they felt someone touch them on the shoulder and they heard the voice of Jesus, saying, "Arise, and fear not."

They lifted up their heads and looked around. The cloud had disappeared. Moses was gone and so was Elias. Jesus stood there alone.

They started down from the top of the mountain. On the way Jesus said to them, "Do not tell anyone what you saw until I shall be risen from the dead."

MARTHA AND MARY

Bethany was a beautiful city near Jerusalem. It was not far from the Mount of Olives. Jesus went to Bethany very often. It was quiet and restful, and his very good friends, Mary, Martha and Lazarus, lived there. He often went to their home to rest after He had been working hard. There was always joy and happiness when Jesus came. Martha and Mary and Lazarus did everything they could for him.

One day when Jesus was visiting in Bethany, Mary sat at His feet and listened to every word He spoke. Martha, her sister, was very busy preparing dinner. When she saw Mary sitting at the feet of Jesus, she said, "Lord have You no care that my sister has left me alone to prepare the dinner? Speak to her and tell her to help me."

But Jesus said, "Martha, Martha, you are careful and troubled about many things. But, only one thing is important. Mary has chosen the better part. It shall not be taken away from her."

THE STORY OF THE OUR FATHER

Jesus often spoke to His disciples about prayer. He said, "Whatever you ask in My name shall be given to you. Ask and you shall receive. Seek and you shall find. Knock and it shall be opened to you."

Jesus Himself prayed much. The disciples often saw Him praying. They wished that they could pray as he prayed. One day they said to Him, "Lord, teach us how to pray." Jesus said, "When you pray you shall say:

"Our Father, Who art in Heaven;
Hallowed be Thy name;
Thy Kingdom come;
Thy will be done on earth as it is in Heaven;
Give us this day our daily bread;
And forgive us our trespasses as we forgive those
who trespass against us
And lead us not into temptation, but deliver us
from evil."

We know this prayer as the Lord's Prayer because it was given to us by Jesus Himself. In this prayer Jesus Himself teaches us what we ought to pray for.

It was evening. All day long Jesus had been teaching the people and healing the sick that had been brought to Him. Now He was tired out and He sat down to rest.

A little crowd of women came up to Him, bringing with them their children. Some mothers carried babies in their arms. There were little boys and girls who held fast to their mother's hand. There were older children who ran on ahead and crowded around our blessed Lord. The children had heard so many wonderful things about Jesus that they wanted to see Him and talk to Him. Their mothers hoped that Jesus would lay His hands upon their little ones and bless them so that they would grow up to be good.

The disciples knew that the Savior was tired out and they were afraid that the children would bother Him. They told the mothers to take their children away. They had forgotten that Jesus had once said to them, "He that shall receive one such little child in My name, receives Me."

When Jesus saw what was happening He said to His disciples, "Let the little children come to Me and do not forbid them, for in their innocence they are like the angels in the Kingdom of Heaven."

You can imagine how glad the children were and how happy it made their mothers to see them crowding round Jesus while He blessed them and spoke to them.

JESUS ENTERS JERUSALEM

It was now three years since Jesus had left Nazareth. He had traveled all over the country, preaching to the people, healing the sick, raising the dead to life and forgiving sinners. It was now time for Him to finish His work. He had come to open Heaven for us by dying on the cross.

The feast of the Pasch was near at hand. Jesus and His disciples went to Jerusalem. A great crowd of people followed them. As they drew near to the city, Jesus sent two of His disciples on ahead. "Just before you come to the city," He said, "there is little village. As you enter the village, you shall find a young ass tied at the door. Untie it and bring it to Me. If anyone says anything to you, say to him, 'The Master has need of it.'"

The disciples did as Jesus commanded them. They found the ass. While they were unfastening it the owner ran up and said, "Why do you untie the ass?" They answered, "The Master has need of it." The owner let them take the ass. They brought the animal back to Jesus and spread their cloaks on it and Jesus sat on its back.

As they came near to Jerusalem, a great crowd came out from the city to meet them. They spread their garments on the ground in front of Jesus. They cut down branches from the palms that grew near and laid them before His path. They began to sing in a great chorus, "Blessed is He that comes in the name of the Lord! Hosanna to the Son of David."

Little boys and girls, grown men and women, all waved their palm branches and spread their garments on the ground and sang their song of praise as Jesus passed.

JESUS CLEARS THE TEMPLE

When Jesus reached Jerusalem, He went to the Temple. He saw that the house of God was filled with merchants money-changers carrying on their businesses. He became very angry and cast them out of the Temple saying, "My house is a house of prayer, but you have made it a den of thieves."

THE WIDOW'S OFFERING

Everywhere Jesus went in Jerusalem, He talked to the people about God and taught them many new

things. This filled the priests and chief officials of the Jews with envy.

One day, Jesus was sitting in the Temple and He noticed a poor widow who had just put two small coins in the collection bowl. Calling his disciples, Jesus said, "This poor woman has put in more than all those who had been giving money to the Temple. The others have put in what they could afford, but she put in all she has to live on."

As Jesus preached and taught the people, the Jewish officials became more and more angry. They even heard the children calling in the streets and in the Temple, "Hosanna to the Son of David," so they came to Jesus and told Him to make the children keep still, but Jesus answered, "Have you not read that out of the mouths of children comes the highest praise?"

They did not answer His question.

SUGGESTIONS FOR STUDY

I. UNDERLINE THE CORRECT ANSWER.

a. Martha had a sister named (Esther—Mary—Lazarus).
b. Jesus let (John—Andrew—Peter) walk on the water.
c. The prodigal son returned to his (mother's—sister's—father's) house.
d. Jesus called (James—Nathanael—Peter) a rock.
e. Jesus took Peter, James and (Philip—Matthew—John) up on the mountain.

2. FILL IN THE BLANKS WITH THESE WORDS.

Lazarus   prodigal   walked   two   Elias   coins
five   lost   storm   Samaritan

a. Jesus quieted the _____ at sea.
b. A great crowd was fed with _____ loaves and _____ fishes.
c. Jesus _____ on the water.
d. Moses and _____ appeared on the mountain with Jesus and the three apostles.
e. _____ was the brother of Martha and Mary.
f. The shepherd went out to look for his _____ sheep.
g. The _____ helped the man who was robbed.
h. The father waited for his _____ son to come home.
i. The widow put two _____ in the collection.

3. HOW WELL CAN YOU THINK?

a. The Our Father is the Lord's prayer because it was taught by Jesus Himself. What four things do we ask of God in the Our Father?
b. The good Shepherd did everything he could to find his lost sheep. To what lengths did Jesus go in order to open the gates of Heaven?
c. Jesus told the people what they should do to become holy. Many of these things were said in the Sermon on the Mount. Which is your favorite saying of Jesus in this sermon? Why is it your favorite saying?

4. CAN YOU USE THESE WORDS IN SENTENCES?

amazed	husks	disappear
reproach	rejoice	merchants
rough	prodigal	envy
important	persecute	parable

XVIII † THE SUFFERINGS AND DEATH OF OUR LORD

It was Thursday, the
day before Jesus died. One of His friends in Jerusalem
had made ready a large room upstairs in his house
where Jesus and His disciples could celebrate the feast
of the Pasch. Jesus sent Peter and John there to prepare the Paschal supper. They bought wine and un-
leavened bread and wild lettuce. They prepared the
Paschal lamb as required by the Law of Moses. They
carried all of these things into the large upper room
and returned to Jesus.

When it was night, Jesus and His twelve apostles
went to the upper room. He took His place at the
table among the apostles. He said to them, "Long have
I desired to eat this Pasch with you before I die."

Then Jesus and His apostles ate the Paschal supper
and did everything that the Law of Moses commanded. They said prayers and sang hymns and Jesus

told them about the first Pasch when God spared the first-born of the Israelites and when Moses led the Children of Israel out of Egypt.

When the Paschal supper was over, Jesus rose and poured water into a large basin. Then He took a towel and began to wash the feet of His apostles.

Simon Peter was shocked when Jesus came to wash his feet. He said, "Lord, do You wash my feet?"

"You do not know what I am doing," Jesus answered, "but you shall know hereafter."

Simon Peter said, "You shall never wash my feet."

Jesus answered, "If I do not wash your feet, you shall not have any part with Me."

When Simon Peter heard this, he cried out to Jesus, "Lord, wash not only my feet but also my hands and my head."

After He had finished washing the feet of the apostles, Jesus sat down with them again and said, "I have given you an example. As I have done to you, so do to one another."

Then He told them that one of the Twelve would betray Him. They did not believe that such a thing could be possible. They began to ask, "Is it I, Lord?"

Jesus told them that before the next morning they would all run away from Him. "It is written," He said, " 'I will strike the shepherd, and the sheep of the flock shall be scattered.' "

Peter said to Him, "Even if all the others run away from You, I will never leave You."

Jesus said to him, "I say to you that this night, before the cock crows twice, you will deny Me thrice."

John, who was sitting very close to Jesus at the table, asked, "Lord, who is it that will betray You?"

Jesus answered, "It is he to whom I shall hand the piece of bread dipped in wine."

Then Jesus dipped a piece of bread in wine and handed it to Judas Iscariot. Judas took it and said, "Is it I, Lord?"

Jesus said to him, "You have said it."

As soon as Jesus spoke, Judas left the room.

And now the moment for which Jesus had waited so long had come. He took bread and blessed it and broke it and gave it to His disciples, saying, "Take and eat; This is My Body."

Then He took the cup with wine in it and said, "Take and Drink; This is My Blood which shall be shed for you and for many unto the remission of sins. As often as you shall do these things, you shall do them in memory of Me."

With these words Jesus changed the bread and wine into His Body and Blood.

Thus it was that our Lord said the First Mass. He then gave His apostles Holy Communion.

Jesus spoke words of greatest love to His apostles when the First Mass was over. "Little children," He said, "I am going away and you cannot come where I am going. Love one another as I have loved you. I am going away to prepare a place for you. I will come again and take you with Me so that where I am you may be."

THE AGONY IN THE GARDEN

Jesus left the supper room. The apostles followed their Master. They went through the streets silently

and, passing out of the gates of the city, they went toward the Mount of Olives. At last they came to a little garden that was called Gethsemani. It was then almost midnight.

Jesus said to His apostles, "Sit here while I go yonder and pray." Then He took Peter, James and John and went into the garden. A great sadness came over Him. He became afraid. He said to the three apostles. "My soul is sad even unto death; wait here and watch."

Jesus went on a little way and threw Himself upon the ground. He prayed, "O My father, if it be possible, let this cup pass from Me; yet not My will but Thine be done."

Jesus thought of all the terrible pain that He should have to suffer. The next day He would die on the cross. He thought of all those who would turn away from Him. He began to perspire, and His sweat became like drops of blood which fell to the ground.

After a long time, Jesus got up and looked for Peter, James and John. They were sound asleep. He awakened them and said, "Why do you sleep? Arise and pray lest you enter into temptation."

The Savior went back and prayed again to His Father. "Father, if it be possible let this chalice pass from Me; yet not My will but Thine be done."

Again He returned to the three apostles. They were sound asleep. This time He did not awaken them.

A third time Jesus went back to pray as before.

He came again to His apostles and found them still asleep. "Sleep now and take your rest," He said. "The hour has come when the Son of Man is betrayed into the hands of sinners. Rise, let us go. Behold, who will betray Me is at hand."

JUDAS' KISS

While Jesus was still speaking, there was a great noise in the distance. They could hear the sound of many voices shouting and calling to one another. Suddenly, they saw a great crowd of people carrying lanterns and torches and coming toward the garden. Many of them had clubs and swords. Judas Iscariot walked at the head of them.

As soon as Judas saw Jesus in the darkness, he walked up to Him and said, "Hail, Rabbi." Then He kissed Jesus. Before that, he had told the crowd, "The One that I shall kiss is He. Lay hold of Him and lead Him away."

Jesus said to Judas, "Friend, do you betray the Son of Man with a kiss?" Then He turned to the crowd and said to them very gently, "Whom do you seek?"

They answered, "Jesus of Nazareth."

Jesus said, "I am He."

When Jesus spoke, the people in the crowd became frightened. They drew back and some fell to the ground in fright.

A second time Jesus asked, "Whom do you seek?"

They said, "Jesus of Nazareth."

Jesus said, "I have told you that I am He. If you seek Me, let these others go their way."

Jesus did not want the crowd to harm His apostles. But Simon Peter made up his mind to fight for his Master. He pulled out his sword and cut off the ear of a man whose name was Malchus. Jesus said to him, "Put your sword away. Do you not know that if I ask My father He will send a whole army of angels?" Then He touched the ear of Malchus and healed it.

Jesus turned once more to the crowd and said, "You have come with clubs and swords to take Me prisoner. When I was with you every day in the Temple, you did not lay hands on Me. But it is so that the scriptures may be fulfilled."

There were some soldiers in the crowd and they took hold of Jesus and bound Him with cords. Then they led Him away to the house of the high priest. The apostles ran away. They left their Master in the hands of His enemies. Only Peter and John followed Him, but from a long way off.

It was very, very late when the crowd brought Jesus to Annas, the father-in-law of Caiphas, the high priest. John followed them into the great yard of the palace. He saw Peter standing outside the gate. He spoke to the woman who had charge of the gate and she let Peter in. There was a fire burning in the middle of the yard for the servants and the soldiers to warm themselves. Peter went up to the fire. A maid-servant was standing there and she looked at Peter and said, "You were with Jesus of Nazareth. Are you not one of his disciples?"

Peter said, "I do not understand what you are saying." Just then a cock crowed.

Meanwhile, Jesus had been brought before Annas. Annas asked Him about His teaching. Jesus said to him, "I have always spoken openly to the world. Ask those who have heard Me what I have taught."

When Jesus had spoken these words an attendant who was standing by His side struck Him on the cheek and said, "Is that the way You answer?"

JESUS AND CAIPHAS

Annas sent Jesus to the high priest, whose name was Caiphas. Caiphas and all the priests and scribes were waiting for Him. They had made up their minds to have Jesus put to death, but they could not prove that He had done anything wrong. A number of men got up and made charges against Jesus, but they could not prove that what they said was true.

Then Caiphas stood up and said to Jesus, "Are You the Christ, the Son of God?"

Jesus answered calmly, "I am."

Caiphas was filled with rage. He tore his garments in anger and said, "We do not need more witnesses. You heard Him say that He is the Son of God. He has blasphemed. What shall we do with Him?"

They all cried out that he must die.

While all this was going on, Peter was still waiting outside in the courtyard. Soon another servant spoke to him and said, "Were you not with Jesus?"

A second time Peter said, "I do not know the Man. I am not one of His disciples."

Later another man came up and said, "Surely you were one of His disciples." Peter then began to curse and swear and say that he did not know Jesus.

Just then the cock crowed again. The soldiers were leading Jesus out of the palace and across the yard. Jesus passed close to where Peter was standing. He looked at Peter.

Then Peter remembered the words of the Master,

"Before the cock crows twice, you will deny Me thrice." He was ashamed of himself and his heart was breaking. He went out and wept bitterly. He always remembered his shameful denial of Jesus.

That night they kept our Lord in prison. Rough soldiers beat Him. They spat on Him and struck Him in the face. They made fun of Him. They treated Him worse than a wicked criminal. Some of the soldiers blindfolded Jesus. Then they struck Him with the palms of their hands and said, "Tell us, O Christ, who it is that struck You."

JESUS AND PILATE

The next morning Caiphas ordered the soldiers to bring Jesus to Pilate, the Roman governor. The high priest had no right to condemn a man to death. Only the Roman governor could do that. The lawyers of the high priest told Pilate that Jesus should be put to death. A great crowd of people out in the street cried out, "Crucify Him, crucify Him!"

But Pilate said, "He is innocent. I do not see what wrong He has done, but if you want me to, I will scourge Him and then set Him free."

The Roman soldiers took Jesus and tied Him to a pillar. Then they took whips and beat Him. They

beat Him until His body was covered with blood. After this they put a purple cloak around Him. They made a crown of thorns and put it on His head. Then they placed a reed in His hands and called in all of the soldiers who were not on duty. They all stood around Jesus and made fun of Him. They knelt down before Him and said, "Hail, King of the Jews." They spat upon Him and struck Him.

JESUS IS CONDEMNED TO DEATH

Dressed in the purple cloak and crowned with thorns, Jesus was led back to Pilate. When Pilate saw

Him, he felt sorry for Him. He brought Jesus out in front of the palace and showed Him to the crowd. He said to them, "Behold the Man."

But the chief priests and the people became more angry. They shouted, "Crucify Him, crucify Him!"

Pilate said to the people, "How can I crucify Him when He has done nothing wrong?"

The people answered, "He must die according to our law because He made Himself the Son of God."

Pilate saw that he was doing no good and he was afraid there would be a riot. So he told a servant to bring him a basin and a pitcher of water. The servant poured the water over Pilate's hands and Pilate said to the people, "I am innocent of the blood of this just man; see to it yourselves."

The people cried out, "His blood be upon us and upon our children!"

Then Pilate delivered Jesus to the people to be crucified. The soldiers took the purple cloak off Jesus and gave Him back His own garments. Then they placed a heavy cross upon His shoulders and led Him away to be crucified. He carried His cross through the streets of the city and outside the walls to a hill that was called Calvary. Two thieves who had been condemned to death went with Him, carrying their crosses.

The soldiers were afraid that Jesus would not have strength enough to carry His cross the whole way, so they seized a man named Simon who had just come in from the country and forced him to help Jesus carry His cross. When they reached the top of Calvary, the soldiers stripped Jesus of His garments and stretched Him on the cross. They fastened Him to the cross by driving large nails through His hands and His feet. Then they raised the cross with Jesus on it.

Jesus said, "Father, forgive them, for they know not what they do."

They also crucified the two thieves, one of them on the right of Jesus and one of them on the left.

JESUS DIES ON THE CROSS

For three hours Jesus hung on the cross. The thief on His right hand said to Him, "Lord, remember me when You come into Your Kingdom."

Jesus said to him, "This day you shall be with Me in Paradise."

Mary, His Mother, and John, His apostle, stood at the foot of the cross of Jesus. Jesus looked down at them and said to His Mother, "Woman, behold your son!" Then He said to John, "Son, behold your Mother!"

Jesus was dying. There was no one to help Him. Even His Father in Heaven seemed far away. He cried out, "My God, My God, why have You forsaken Me?"

Jesus had lost much blood. He was burning up with fever. He cried out, "I thirst!"

A soldier dipped a sponge in sour wine and, sticking it on the tip of his spear, pressed it against the Savior's lips. Jesus tasted it and turned His head.

At about three o'clock in the afternoon, Jesus cried out with a loud voice, "It is finished." Then He said, "Father, into your hands I commend My spirit!" and died.

All at once it became dark as night. The earth shook. Great rocks were broken apart. The graves

opened and many of the dead came to life. When the officer of the Roman soldiers saw all this, he said, "Surely, this man was the Son of God."

In order to be sure that Jesus was dead, one of the soldiers took his lance and pierced the Savior's side. A stream of blood and water poured out. Jesus had shed the last drop of His blood for sinners.

THE BURIAL OF JESUS

Nicodemus and Joseph of Arimathea were disciples of Jesus. They were rich men and held high offices in Jerusalem. They did not let anyone know that they were followers of Jesus. They were afraid that they might lose their high positions.

But after Jesus was dead, they gained courage. Joseph went to Pilate and asked him for the body of the Savior. They took the body down from the cross and wrapped it in fine linens. They placed spices, which Nicodemus brought, in the folds of the linen. Then they put the body in a new grave which belonged to Joseph, and rolled a large stone in front of the entrance. This grave was in a garden. The next day the Jews put some soldiers at the tomb to guard it. They feared that the apostles would come and steal the body of Jesus.

SUGGESTIONS FOR STUDY

1. WHO ARE WE?

   a. We took hold of Jesus and bound Him with cords.
   b. We ran away and left Jesus in the hands of His enemies.
   c. We shouted out "Crucify Him."
   d. We were crucified with Jesus.
   e. We were present at the Last Supper.

2. WHO SAID THIS?

   a. "Take and eat; This is My Body."
   b. "Surely, this Man was the Son of God!"
   c. "I do not know the Man; I am not one of His disciples."
   d. "Lord, remember me when You come into Your Kingdom."
   e. "Lord, who is it that will betray You?"

3. FILL IN THE BLANKS WITH THESE WORDS.

   apostles　　pain　　turn　　Communion　　Body　　Blood

   a. At the Last Supper, Jesus changed the bread and wine into His ——————— and ———————.
   b. The apostles received their first Holy ——————— at the Last Supper.
   c. In the Garden of Gethsemani, Jesus was sad because He thought of all the terrible ——————— He would have to suffer.
   d. Jesus also thought of all those who would ——————— away from Him.
   e. The three ——————— fell asleep while Jesus prayed in the garden.

4. MATCH COLUMN I WITH COLUMN II.

   - a. Pilate　　　　( ) stood by the cross.

b. Caiphas   ( ) beat Jesus, crowned Him with thorns, and spat on Him.

c. Soldiers   ( ) was struck by an attendant.

d. John   ( ) was afraid there would be a riot.

e. Jesus   ( ) said that Jesus blasphemed.

5. HOW WELL CAN YOU THINK?

a. Peter denied Jesus and committed a great sin; yet Peter became a great saint. How did this happen?

b. While hanging on the cross Jesus said, "Father, forgive them, for they know not what they do." How can we be like Jesus in this way?

c. What great wrong did Pilate do because he was afraid? What should we do when we are afraid?

6. DO YOU KNOW WHAT THESE WORDS MEAN?

traitor	unleavened	riot
betray	deny	blaspheme
attendant	thrice	courtyard

XIX † THE
RISEN LIFE
OF OUR LORD

Early in the morning on the third day after Jesus was buried, there was a great earthquake. An angel came down from Heaven and rolled back the stone from the entrance of the grave. His face was bright as the sun and his garments were white as snow. When the guards that had been placed at the tomb saw all this they fainted with fear.

When the sun had risen, Mary Magdalen and other pious women came to the grave in order to put more spices in it. On the way, they said to one another, "Who shall roll back the stone for us, for it is very large?"

When they came to the grave, they saw the stone rolled back. They went inside, but the body of Jesus was not there.

They could not understand what had happened. Suddenly they saw two angels, who said to them,

"Fear not, you seek Jesus Who was crucified. He is not here. He has risen. Come and see the place where His body was laid. Then, go quickly. Tell His disciples that He has risen. You shall see Him in Galilee as He told you."

Mary Magdalen left the grave and ran as fast as she could to tell the disciples. Peter and John hurried to the grave. They saw the linen cloths in which the body had been wrapped, but the body of Jesus was not there. They went away wondering what had happened.

Mary Magdalen had come back to the tomb. She did not know whether or not the angels that she had seen were real. Suddenly, she saw a man standing there and thought that he was the one who took care of the garden. She was weeping. The man said to her, "Woman, why do you weep? Whom are you seeking?"

She said to Him, "Sir, if you have taken Him from this place, tell me where you have laid Him and I will take Him away." The man said to her, "Mary!"

Mary looked up and saw that it was really Jesus. She fell on her knees and said, *"Rabboni*, Master."

Jesus said to her, "Do not touch Me, but go to My disciples and tell them that I ascend to My Father and to your Father, to My God and to your God."

JESUS ASCENDS INTO HEAVEN

Jesus remained on earth for forty days. During that time, He appeared to His disciples many times. He allowed Thomas to put his finger into the wounds of His hands and to put his hand into the wound in His side, to prove that He had really risen from the dead. He gave them many other proofs of His resurrection.

Once, when He appeared to them, He said, "Receive the Holy Ghost. Whose sins you shall forgive, they are forgiven them. Whose sins you shall retain, they are retained." With these words Jesus instituted the Sacrament of Penance.

On the fortieth day after His resurrection, Jesus appeared to His apostles when they were all together in Jerusalem. He told them that He would send them the Holy Ghost, Who would help them to preach the Gospel and tell people about Jesus.

After Jesus had told them this, He led them out to Mount Olivet. When they reached there, He said to them, "All power is given to Me in Heaven and in earth. Go, therefore, teach all nations, baptizing them in the name of the Father and of the Son and of the Holy Ghost. And, behold, I am with you always even to the end of the world."

Jesus then lifted up His hands and blessed them. While they were looking, He was raised up and a cloud took Him out of their sight. Two angels in white garments appeared to them and said, "You men of Galilee, why stand you looking up to Heaven? This Jesus Who was taken up from you into Heaven shall so come again."

The disciples adored God and went back to Jerusalem with great joy.

THE DESCENT OF THE HOLY GHOST

For ten days after our Lord had ascended into Heaven, the apostles and disciples waited in the upper

room where Jesus had eaten the Last Supper. The Blessed Virgin was with them and they spent the time in prayer. They were getting their hearts ready for the Holy Ghost Whom Jesus had promised to send.

One day Saint Peter rose up and told them that a new apostle would have to be appointed to take the place of Judas. There were two men among them who had been with our Savior from the beginning. They were Joseph, called Barsabas, and Matthias. The choice lay between these two. All who were in the room now joined in prayer, and lots were cast to see which one God wanted. The lot fell upon Matthias and he was numbered among the apostles.

On the tenth day they heard a mighty sound from heaven. It was like a great wind and it filled the house and was even heard in the street. Then there appeared over each one of them little tongues of fire and they were all filled with the Holy Ghost. This day is called Pentecost, and is the day on which the Church began her missionary work.

After the disciples were filled with the Holy Ghost, they went out as missionaries to preach to all the nations of the earth. They worked miracles and converted many to the teachings of Jesus. Before the apostles died, they appointed successors who were to take their places and carry on to the end of the world the work that Jesus had begun.

SUGGESTIONS FOR STUDY

1. WHO SAID THIS AND TO WHOM?

   a. "Whose sins you shall forgive, they are forgiven them."
   b. "Fear not, you seek Jesus Who was crucified. He is not here."
   c. "Who shall roll back the stone for us?"

2. WHO AM I?

   a. I was appointed to take Judas' place.
   b. I ascended into heaven.
   c. I put my fingers into the wounds in Jesus' hands and side.
   d. I was in the upper room with the apostles and disciples when the Holy Ghost came.
   e. I told the apostles to "Go, teach all nations."

3. FILL IN THE BLANKS WITH THE CORRECT WORDS.

angels   forty   guards   Pentecost   Christ

a. The _____ fainted away with fear.
b. The women did not find the body of Jesus in the grave, but they did see two _____.
c. Mary Magdalen thought that _____ was the man who took care of the garden.
d. Jesus remained on earth _____ days after His Resurrection.
e. _____ is the day the Church began its missionary work.

4. DRAW A LINE UNDER THE CORRECT ANSWER.

a. When Jesus said "Whose sins, etc.", He instituted the sacrament of (Penance—Holy Eucharist).
b. Jesus told the (apostles—women) that He would be with them until the end of the world.
c. The Holy Ghost came on the (eighth—tenth) day after Jesus ascended into heaven.
d. (John—Peter) said that a new apostle would have to be appointed in the place of Judas.

5. HOW WELL CAN YOU THINK?

a. Before the apostles died, they appointed successors to take their places. Who are the successors of the apostles now?
b. The angels told the disciples that Jesus shall come again as they had seen Him going into heaven. What did the angels mean?

6. CAN YOU USE THESE WORDS IN SENTENCES?

fortieth	appear	successors
instituted	retained	missionary
seek	resurrection	ascend

INDEX, GLOSSARY
AND PRONOUNCING GUIDE

ā *as in* dāte   th *as in* thin   ẽ *as in* makẽr   ū *as in* ūse

ă *as in* ăm   th *as in* then   ī *as in* bīte   ŭ *as in* ŭp

â *as in* fâre   tū *as in* pictūre   ĭ *as in* bĭt   û *as in* bûrn

à *as in* àsk   ē *as in* bē   ō *as in* hōpe   o͞o *as in* fo͞od

à *as in* àbout   ĕ *as in* mĕt   ŏ *as in* hŏt   o͝o *as in* fo͝ot

ä *as in* fär   ē *as in* hēre   ô *as in* lôrd   ou *as in* out

Aaron (âr'ŭn), brother of Moses; first high priest of the Israelites, 92, 93-96, 107, 109, 114, 115.

Abel (ā'bĕl), a son of Adam and Eve, 12-13.

Abram (ā'brăm), Abraham's name before God changed it, 23-26.

Abraham (ā'bră-hăm), a great patriarch; father of the Chosen People, 22-34, 36, 38, 89, 172.

Achab (ā'kăb), a king of the Israelites, 139-140, 141.

Adam (ăd'ăm), the first man, 3-12.

Alpheus (ăl-fē'ŭs), father of James, the Apostle, 209.

Amalecites (ăm'à-lek-īts), enemies of the Israelites, 107.

Aman (à'măn), a prince of Babylon who hated the Israelites, 164-169.

Andrew (ăn'dro͞o), one of the twelve apostles, 203, 204, 205, 208, 209.

Anna (ăn'à), mother of Samuel, 127.

Anna (ăn'à), the holy prophetess who met the Holy Family in the Temple, 187.

Annas (ăn-năs'), father-in-law of Caiphas, 251.

Anoint (à-noint'), to set apart by pouring oil on a person or thing as a sign of authorization, 130, 131.

Apostles (à-pŏs'l'z), the twelve disciples chosen by Christ to help Him teach; the first bishops of the Church, 209.

Assuerus (ă-sū-ē'rŭs), a king of Persia, the husband of Esther, 163-169.

Assyrians (ă-sĭr'ĭ-ănz), a people who captured the Israelites, 147-148.

Augustus (à-gŭs'tŭs), the Roman emperor at the time of Christ's birth, 182, 183.

Baal (bā'ăl), a false god, 122, 140, 141-142.

Babylon (băb'ĭ-lŏn), capital of Babylonia, an empire in West Asia, 155, 156, 158.

Barsabus (bär-să'bŭs), a disciple of Jesus, 267.

Bartholomew (bär-thŏl'ō-mū) (see *Nathanael.*)

Beatitudes, the Eight (bē-ăt'ĭ-tūd), the sayings spoken by Jesus in the Sermon on the Mount, 222-223.

Benjamin (bĕn'jȧ-mĭn), youngest son of Jacob, 57, 58, 70, 72, 73, 74, 75, 77.

Bethel (bĕth'ĕl), the place where Jacob had his dream, 48.

Bethany (bĕth'ȧ-nĭ), the town of Mary, Martha and Lazarus, 234.

Bethlehem (bĕth'lē-ĕm), the town where Jesus was born, 183-190.

Bullock (bŏŏl'ŭk), an ox, 141-143.

Butler, the chief (bŭt'lēr), one of the men for whom Joseph interpreted a dream, 62-64.

Cain (kān), a son of Adam and Eve, 12-14.

Caiphas (kā'ĭ-făs), the high priest who accused Jesus, 251-253.

Caleb (kā'lĕb), one of the scouts sent to explore the Promised Land, 114, 115.

Calvary (kăl'vȧ-rĭ), the place where Jesus was crucified, 255-259.

Cana (kā'nȧ), a town in Galilee, 205, 206, 209.

Capharnaum (kȧ'fär-nȧ-ŭm), a town in Galilee, 210, 211.

Carmel, Mount (kär'mĕl), the place where Elias offered sacrifice to God, 141.

Centurion, the (sĕn-tū'rĭ-ŭn), the Roman captain who asked Jesus to heal his servant, 210-211.

Chanaan (kā'năn), the Promised Land of the Israelites, 23-24, 34, 51-52, 69, 75, 77, 79, 113, 117, 121-122.

Chef, the chief (shĕf), one of the men for whom Joseph interpreted a dream, 62-64.

Commandments, Ark of the (kŏ-mȧnd'mĕnts) (see *Covenant, Ark of the.*)

Commandments, the Ten (kŏ-mȧnd'mĕnts), the ten laws given by God to the Israelites, 107-112.

Covenant (kŭv'ĕ-nănt), an agreement made between two persons, 26, 135.

Covenant, Ark of the (kŭv'ĕ-nănt), the chest in which the Commandments were kept, 112, 127, 128.

Daniel (dăn'yĕl), a great prophet of the Jews, 154-160.

Darius (dȧ-rī'ŭs), a king of Babylon, 158-160.

David (dā'vĭd), a great king of the Israelites, 131-135.

David, House of (dā'vĭd), the royal family from which Jesus sprang, 183.

Devil, the (dĕv''l), the Evil One, 8-10, 201-202.

Disciples (dĭ-sī'p'lz), a follower of Christ, 209.

Dothian (dō-thĭ'ăn), an area located in Palestine, 59.

Dove (dŭv), a small pigeon, 19, 20.

Dumb (dŭm), to be unable to speak, 179.

Elcana (ĕl'kä-nä), father of Samuel, 127.

Elias (ē-lī'ăs), a great prophet of the Israelites, 139-143, 232-234.

Eliezer (ĕl-ĭ-ē'zēr), the servant of Abraham, 34-38.

Elizabeth (ē-lĭz'ȧ-beth), cousin of the Blessed Virgin Mary, 177-182, 199.

Egypt (ē'jĭpt), one of the great kingdoms of the ancient world, 60, 65-68, 71-103.

Egypt, Plagues of (ē'jĭpt plāgz), the troubles and sufferings sent by God upon the Egyptians, 93-99.

Ephraim, Tribe of (ē′frā-ĭm), one of two tribes formed by the division of the tribe of Joseph, 121.

Esau (ē′sô), the brother of Jacob, 40-46, 51-54.

Esther (ĕs′tẽr), a queen of Persia, 162-169.

Eve (ēv), the first woman, 8-12.

Famine (făm′ĭn), a lack of food, 66-68.

Frankincense (frăngk′ĭn-sĕns), a sweet-smelling gummy substance used in making incense, 189.

Gabelus (găb′ē-lŭs), a friend of the elder Tobias, 148-151.

Gabriel (gā′brĭ-ĕl), an angel of God, 178-181.

Galilee (găl′ĭ-lē), an area located in Palestine, 191, 204, 205, 206, 264, 266.

Galilee, Sea of (găl′ĭ-lē), a large lake located in Palestine, 207, 227, 230.

Gallows (găl′ōz), a frame on which criminals are hanged, 169.

Gedeon (gĕd′ē-ŏn), a great Jewish warrior, 122-124.

Gessen (gĕs′ĕn), the land given by the Egyptian king to Jacob and his sons, 76, 78.

God, the Father (gŏd), the First Person of the Blessed Trinity, 3-173.

Goliath (gō-lī′ăth), the giant of the Philistines, 131-134.

Governor (gŭv′ẽr-nẽr), a man who rules as the representative of a king, 68, 156, 253.

Haran (hā′răn), a place where Abraham, and later Laban, lived, 23, 46, 51.

Hearth (härth), the part of an oven or fireplace used for cooking, 27.

Hebrew (hē′brōō), an Israelite; the language which the Israelites spoke, 64, 90, 95, 101.

Hebron (hē′brŏn), the place in Palestine where Abraham, Isaac and Jacob were buried, 25, 38, 54, 59.

Heir (âr), the son who inherits his father's property, usually the eldest son, 42.

Heli (hē′lī), a priest who cared for Samuel, 127-129.

Herod (hĕr′ŭd), a king of the Jews, 188-191.

Holy Ghost, the (gōst), the Third Person of the Blessed Trinity, 201, 265-268.

Holy Innocents, the (ĭn′ŏ-sĕnt), the children killed by King Herod, 190.

Holy Spirit, the (spĭr′ĭt) (see *Holy Ghost, the.*)

Horeb, Mount (hôr′eb), (see *Sinai, Mount.*)

Hur (hŭr), one of the helpers of Moses, 107, 109.

Incense (ĭn′sĕns), spices and gums that are mixed together and which give off a pleasant odor when burned, 177.

Isaac (ī′zăk), the son of Abraham, 30-38, 40-46, 54.

Isaias (ī-zā′yăs), a great prophet of the Israelites, 139.

Israel (ĭz′râ-ĕl), the name given to Jacob by an angel, 53, 83.

Israelites (ĭz′rā-ĕl-ītz), the descendants of Jacob (Israel), 83.

Israel, Kingdom of (ĭz′râ-ĕl), one of the two kingdoms of the Hebrews, 135.

Jacob (jā′kŭb), a patriarch of the Israelites, the son of Isaac, 40-54, 57-59, 61, 172.

James (jāmz), brother of John, and one of the twelve Apostles, 208, 209, 232, 247-248.

James (jāmz), son of Alpheus, and one of the twelve Apostles, 209.

Jeremias (jĕr-ē-mī′ăs), a great prophet of the Israelites, 139.

Jeroboam (jĕr-ō-bō′ăm), the first King of Israel, 135.

Jerusalem (jĕ-rōō′sà-lĕm), the capital of the Kingdom of Juda, and the Temple-city of all Jews, 135, 177, 188, 201, 237-240, 266.

Jesus Christ (jē′zŭs), the Second Person of the Blessed Trinity, 12, 135, 139, 172-173, 176-268.

Jew (jōō), a subject of the Kingdom of Juda, 135.

Jethro (jĕth′rō) (see *Raguel*.)

John (jŏn), brother of James, and one of the twelve Apostles, 203, 204, 208, 209, 232, 243, 245, 247-248, 251, 258, 264.

John, the Baptist (jŏn), cousin of Jesus, 182, 199-201, 232.

Jonathan (jŏn′à-thăn), a son of King Saul, 131.

Jordan, the (jôr′d′n), a river located in Palestine, 24, 117, 118, 200, 203.

Joseph (jō′zĕf) (see *Barsabas*.)

Joseph of Arimathea (ăr-ĭ-mà-thē′à), a disciple of Jesus, 259.

Joseph (jō′zĕf), son of Jacob, 56-79.

Joseph, Saint (jō′zĕf), foster-father of Jesus, 179, 183-195.

Joseph, Tribe of (jō′zĕf), one of the original tribes of Israel, later divided by Joseph's sons, 121.

Josue (jŏs′ū-ē), a great leader of the Israelites, 114, 115, 117, 120-122.

Juda (jōō′dà), a son of Jacob, 60, 72, 75, 79.

Juda, Kingdom of (jōō′dà), one of the two kingdoms of the Hebrews, 135.

Juda, Tribe of (jōō′dà), the main tribe of the original tribes of Israel, 122, 155, 172.

Judas (jōō′dăs), Christ's betrayer, one of the twelve Apostles of Jesus, 209, 246, 249, 267.

Jude (jōōd), one of the twelve Apostles, 209.

Judges (jŭj′ĕz), the men who protected and led the Israelites after they reached Chanaan, 122, 129.

Laban (lā′băn), brother of Rebecca, 36-37, 46, 48-51.

Lazarus (lăz′à-rŭs), a man whom Jesus raised from the dead, 214-215.

Leprosy (lĕp′rō-sĭ), a disease which affects the skin, 91.

Levi, Tribe of (lē′vī), the tribe of Israelites from which the priests were selected, 121.

Levite (lē′vīt), a member of the Tribe of Levi, 114.

Lia (lē′à), older sister of Rachel, 49.

Lot (lŏt), nephew of Abraham, 24-25, 28-30.

Madian (mā′dī-ăn), a country in the Sinai peninsula, 86-88, 122.

Madianites (măd-ī′ăn-ītz), a tribe hostile to the Israelites, 123-124.

Malchus (măl′kŭs), the soldier who was wounded by Peter, 250.

Manasses, Tribe of (mà-năs′ēz), one of two tribes formed by the division of the Tribe of Joseph, 121.

Manna (măn′à), a food by which God fed the Israelites in the desert, 106.

Mardochai (mär′dō-kī), the uncle of Esther, 164-169.

Martha (mär'thȧ), a friend of Jesus, the sister of Mary of Bethany, 214, 234.

Mary of Bethany (mâr'ĭ), a friend of Jesus, the sister of Martha, 214, 234-235.

Mary Magdalen (măg'dȧ-lĕn), a friend of Jesus, 215-218, 263-264.

Mary, the Mother of God (mâr'ĭ), the Mother of Jesus Christ, 177-195, 205, 258, 267.

Mathusala (mȧ-tūs'ȧlȧ), a man who lived many years, 17.

Matthew (măth'ū), one of the twelve Apostles, 209.

Matthias (mȧ'thī-ȧs), the man chosen to take Judas' place as an Apostle, 267.

Messias (mĕ-sī'ȧs) (see *Jesus Christ*.)

Miriam (mĭr'ĭ-am), the sister of Moses, 84-85.

Moses (mō'zĭz), the great leader of the Israelites, 82-119, 232-234.

Myrrh (mûr), a valuable and fragrant gum used in making incense, 189.

Nabuchodonosor (năb-ū-kō-dŏn'ō-sŏr), a king of Babylon, 155, 156, 158.

Nachor (nā'kôr), the brother of Abraham, 36.

Naim (nā'ĭm), a town in Galilee, 213.

Nathanael (nȧ-thăn'ȧ-ĕl), one of the twelve Apostles of Jesus, 204-205, 209.

Nazareth (năz'ȧ-rĕth), the town in which Jesus spent His youth, 183, 191-195, 205, 237.

Nebo, Mount (nē'bō), the mountain from which Moses saw Chanaan, 117.

Nicodemus (nĭk-ō-dē'mŭs), a disciple of Christ, 259, 260.

Noe (nō'ē), the man who, with his family, survived the flood, 16-20.

Noe, Ark of (nō'ē), the boat of Noe, 18-20.

Olivet, Mount (ŏl'ĭ-vĕt), the hill on which Jesus suffered the Agony in the Garden, 234, 247, 266.

Palestine (păl'ĕs-tīn), the present-day name for Chanaan, 23.

Paradise, the Garden of (păr'ȧ-dīs), the home of Adam and Eve before they sinned, 6-12.

Pasch, the (păsk) (see *Passover*.)

Passover (pàs'ō-vĕr), the feast of the Israelites which commemorates God's sparing of their children in Egypt, 98-99, 192-193, 237, 243-244.

Pentecost (pĕn'tē-kŏst), the day on which the Holy Ghost came down upon the Apostles; the birthday of the Church, 268.

Persia (pĕr'shĭ-ȧ), a great empire of the ancient world, 163.

Peter (pē'tĕr), one of the twelve Apostles, and later head of the Church, 203, 204, 205, 207-8, 209, 231-233, 243-245, 247-248, 250-253, 264, 267.

Philip (fĭl'ĭp), one of the twelve Apostles, 204-205, 209, 229.

Philistines (fĭ-lĭs'tĭnz), the enemies of the Israelites, 131-134.

Pilate (pī'lȧt), the Roman governor who turned Jesus over to the Jews, 253-255.

Pitch (pĭch), a black tar used to make boats waterproof, 84.

Prodigal (prŏd'ĭ-găl), a person who wastes money or his own natural gifts, 224.

Promised Land, the (prŏm'ĭst lănd) (see *Chanaan*.)

Prophets, the (prŏf'ĕtz), the great men of the Israelites who reminded the people of the will of God, 139.

Psalms (säms), hymns written by King David, 135.

Putiphar (pū'tǐ-fär), the man who had Joseph thrown into prison, 62.

Rachel (rā'chěl), wife of Jacob, 48-50.

Rages (rā'jēz), a town in which the elder Tobias' friend, Gabelus, lived, 148-150.

Raguel (răg'ŭ-ĕl), father-in-law of Moses, 87, 88, 92.

Raguel (răg'ŭ-ĕl), father-in-law of young Tobias, 150.

Raven (rā'věn), a glossy, black bird, 19.

Rebecca (rē-běk'à), wife of Isaac, 35-38, 41-44, 46, 49.

Redeemer (rē-dēm'ēr) (see *Jesus Christ*.)

Red Sea (rĕd sē), a sea located to the east of Egypt, 100, 105.

Reed (rēd), a tall grass which grows in watery places, 84.

Roboam (rō-bō'ăm), first king of Juda, 135.

Ruben (roō'běn), a son of Jacob, 59-61.

Sackcloth (săk'klŏth), a rough cloth, usually worn as a sign of penance, 164.

Sacrifice (săk'rǐ-fīs), an offering made to God, and then destroyed in some way, 13, 20, 31-33, 90, 141-143.

Samaritan (sà-măr'ǐ-tăn), a native of Samaria in Palestine, 224.

Samuel (săm'ū-ĕl), a judge of the Israelites, 127-131.

Sara (sâr'à), wife of Abraham, 23, 26-27, 30, 38.

Sara (sâr'à), wife of young Tobias, 150-152.

Sarai (sā'rī) (see *Sara, the wife of Abraham*.)

Sarephta, the widow of (sà-rĕf'tà), the widow who fed Elias during a famine, 140-141.

Satan (sā'tăn), the Devil, 201-202.

Saul (sôl), a king of the Israelites, 129-134.

Savior, the (sāv'yēr) (see *Jesus Christ*.)

Scepter (sĕp'tēr), the staff of a king, 166.

Serpent (sûr'pĕnt), a snake, 8.

Seth (sĕth), a son of Adam and Eve, 17.

Sheaf (shēf), a bundle of wheat stalks, 58.

Sichem (sī'kĕm), a town located in Palestine, 24, 59.

Simeon (sĭm'ē-ŏn), the man who met the Holy Family in the Temple, 187.

Simon (sī'mŭn), one of the twelve Apostles, 209.

Simon of Cyrene (sī'mŭn), the man who helped Jesus carry His cross, 256.

Simon Peter (sī'mŭn pē'tēr) (see *Peter*.)

Sinai, Mount (sī'nī), the Mount on which Moses saw the Burning Bush, and where God gave Moses the Ten Commandments, 88, 92, 107, 113.

Sodom (sŏd'ŭm), a city destroyed by God because of its wickedness, 24, 28-30.

Solomon (sŏl'ō-mŭn), a wise king of the Israelites, 135.

Staff (stȧf), a long stick carried in the hand, usually for support, 90.

Synagogue (sĭn'a-gŏg), a local meeting place where the Jews prayed and interpreted the Law of Moses, 192, 210, 212, 214.